T0158813

Glory Girls:

Created to Glorify

Kerry Kavlie

WESTBOW
PRESS®
A DIVISION OF THOMAS NELSON
& ZONDERVAN

Scriptures taken from the Holy Bible, New International Version®, NIV®. Copyright © 1973, 1978, 1984, 2011 by Biblica, Inc.™ Used by permission of Zondervan. All rights reserved worldwide. www.zondervan.com The "NIV" and "New International Version" are trademarks registered in the United States Patent and Trademark Office by Biblica, Inc.™

Scripture quotations are taken from the Holy Bible, New Living Translation, copyright ©1996, 2004, 2007, 2013, 2015 by Tyndale House Foundation. Used by permission of Tyndale House Publishers, Inc., Carol Stream, Illinois 60188. All rights reserved.

Scripture quotations from THE MESSAGE. Copyright © by Eugene H. Peterson 1993, 1994, 1995, 1996, 2000, 2001, 2002. Used by permission of NavPress. All rights reserved. Represented by Tyndale House Publishers, Inc.

Scripture quotations marked (ESV) are from the ESV® Bible (The Holy Bible, English Standard Version®), copyright © 2001 by Crossway, a publishing ministry of Good News Publishers. Used by permission. All rights reserved.

WestBow Press books may be ordered through booksellers or by contacting:

WestBow Press
A Division of Thomas Nelson & Zondervan
1663 Liberty Drive
Bloomington, IN 47403
www.westbowpress.com
1 (866) 928-1240

Because of the dynamic nature of the Internet, any web addresses or links contained in this book may have changed since publication and may no longer be valid. The views expressed in this work are solely those of the author and do not necessarily reflect the views of the publisher, and the publisher hereby disclaims any responsibility for them.

Any people depicted in stock imagery provided by Thinkstock are models, and such images are being used for illustrative purposes only. Certain stock imagery © Thinkstock.

ISBN: 978-1-5127-4829-1 (sc)
ISBN: 978-1-5127-4828-4 (e)

Library of Congress Control Number: 2016910717

Print information available on the last page.

WestBow Press rev. date: 7/21/2016

"…whatever you do,
do it all for the glory of God."

(1 Corinthians 10:31b)

Table of Contents

This book is dedicated to our Heavenly Father and the original "Glory Girls" that met in my home four years ago to study God's Word together. You would have never known by looking at us, but we had endured many trials over the years. We had faced infidelity and extramarital affairs, divorce, the death of a husband, aging loved ones, wayward children, depression, infertility, homelessness, and low self-esteem (just to name a few). One had survived a nearly fatal car accident and another an incurable diagnosis. Although it is no easy task enduring such great trials, they were times rich in opportunities to mature in our faith. However, sometimes the greatest opposition we faced arose during the day-to-day struggles of life. These ladies are a constant reminder to me that we were created to glorify God—no matter what circumstances in which we find ourselves!

A few of these precious ladies are pictured on the front cover (with a few new "Glory Girls" who have been added along the way).

A special thanks to my supportive husband, my parents, my children, and my friends for pushing me out of my comfort zone and not laughing (too hard) as I learn from my mistakes.

Preface

I love how God takes our times of complete and utter brokenness and transforms them into something beautiful. *Glory Girls: Created to Glorify* was written during a time of huge transition for my family. We had just packed up our lives and moved across the country with our two little ones in the weeks prior to the birth of this study. If you have ever made a large move, you know exactly what the next several months entailed. I went from a full steam ahead mentality in my walk with the Lord to slamming on the brakes and coming to a dramatic stop. Instead of looking around me and getting involved in His ministry, I became focused on unpacking, finding new doctors, hooking up our internet, and enrolling my son in school. I remember it being a very lonely time and many tears were shed. I knew that God had called us to move, I just did not know why…yet.

Even though it was not clear at the time, God had a plan. It was a plan so much greater than my husband or I could have ever imagined. During that time of loneliness, I began listening to more sermons online, playing Christian music throughout the day, and digging even deeper into God's Word. I started noticing a pattern. Everything I was reading and hearing was about how God was calling me to bring Him glory—with everything He had already given me. I began to break it down and study for myself what exactly that looked like in each aspect of my life. How could I bring Him glory with my ears? How could He receive glory with my eyes? What about my mind? Before I knew it, seven different concepts began to form. Soon my head was filled with thoughts that tied into these ideas.

I started taking my notes that I had written over the course of several months and compiled them into a study format. By this point, I had become much more involved in the community around me. That very next summer, I invited a large group of women to join me in my home as we unpacked all that God had been revealing to me over the course of the past several months. Our first *Glory Girls* study met for seven amazing weeks. On our final week together, I prayed a big prayer over the ladies. You know the kind of prayer I am talking about. It is the kind they warn you not to pray unless you really mean what you are saying. I prayed that the Lord would take us to the next level in our walk with Him. I asked Him to reveal Himself to us in immeasurable ways that we could not even imagine (Ephesians 3:20).

At the close of our study, I was in awe of everything God had shown me. I had seen firsthand how He was using His Words in Scripture to speak directly to that group of women. Everything seemed so perfect. However, things were about to dramatically change…and change quickly.

Exactly one week to the day of the completion our study, my phone rang late in the evening. It was my daughter's pediatrician. My daughter had been at her routine well check just two days prior, and her blood work was concerning. The pediatrician gently told me that it appeared that her little, 24-month-old body was battling leukemia. Her doctor was hopeful that maybe there had been a mistake since she was not showing any symptoms, but right away I knew it had not been mistake. God was about to reveal Himself in a big way "thanks" to my prayer request the previous week.

The next two-and-a-half years were a whirlwind. Our precious little girl underwent surgery to have her port placed, endured harsh rounds of chemo, survived countless spinal taps, and braved painful bone marrow aspirations. We spent long weeks in the hospital. Our days at home were lived in complete isolation from the outside world as we fought to keep her world free of germs. There were several times that we thought we were going to lose her, but God continued to give her life. In spite of our seemingly dark circumstances, my husband and I could go on and on about the amazing things that God taught our family during that time.

God calls us to live our lives in such a way that when others see how we live, they will praise our Father in Heaven (Matthew 5:16). During our darkest and scariest times, whether we liked it or not, all eyes were on our family. As a result of our trial, we became messengers to hurting families in the hospital. We were able to share our story on multiple news stations and radio programs. Soon our daughter was in magazines and on local billboards. My husband and I were repeatedly asked to speak at different events. Our desire during the process was to be a light where God placed us, even though Satan had every desire to use our circumstances to extinguish our fire for the Lord.

God had been slowly pouring truth into me up until that life-changing call. He had prepared me in advance for the good works He called me to do (Ephesians 2:10). He had filled my mind with His Word from the time I was very little and I did not depart from it (Proverbs 22:6). He used my weaknesses to teach me to rely on His strength (2 Corinthians 12:9). He honored my request to reveal Himself in a big way…much bigger than I could have ever imagined.

It has been four years since the initial unveiling of *Glory Girls*. Since then, the study had been sitting on a shelf, simply collecting dust. It was time for the words in this study to come out of hiding and shine for His glory! God had so much in store for my life that I never saw coming. He has plans for your life as well.

Some of you might feel stuck in a spiritual rut. You know that God is there, but you feel like He is not actively participating in your life. If that is the case, I pray that you would continue to allow God to reveal Himself to you and lovingly remind you know that you are not alone. Use this quiet season to prepare for upcoming trials.

Some (if not most) of you might be in the fire right now (1 Peter 1:6–7). You may be experiencing extreme financial crisis, a wayward child, a death of a loved one, a horrific diagnosis, infertility, or the loss of a job. Unfortunately, it is much easier to prepare for battle when you are not currently *in* the midst of a battle. That being said, if you find yourself in the middle of trial, it is better to start somewhere than not at all. Now is the time to stay in God's Word. Now is the time to plant your feet in truth as Satan will be trying even harder to manipulate your thoughts. You must be consistent and intentional. If you let Him, God will use your current trial to give you wisdom, reveal Himself to you, challenge you to re-think your priorities, give you hope, build character, and even increase your prayer life (James 1:2–4). He will use this battle to strengthen you and prepare you for the road ahead. Trials are a crucial time of sharpening for the believer. Embrace (yes…embrace!) this opportunity to learn more about who God is. What a privilege we have to not only read about Him, but get to see His promises fulfilled firsthand! I pray the completion of this study is not the end of your time in the Word, but just the beginning. Even the smallest, flickering flame can start a fire (James 3:5).

God has carefully brought you to the place where you are today. He has begun a good work in you and He plans on carrying it out until completion (Philippians 1:6). He has never given up on you, nor has He left you (Psalm 37:28). Expect troubles to come, but do not fear them. It is just a result of the sinful world in which we live (John 16:33). Your trials serve a purpose. They are two-fold. They will help burn away your old self and form you into the woman God wants you to be. Most importantly, however, they will allow God a unique opportunity to reveal Himself to not only you, but to the hurting world around you! So in *whatever* you do, in *wherever* you go, and with *whomever* you meet, may you always be a girl who gives God the glory!

Introduction

Today was just an ordinary day for me. At the Kavlie household, we ate breakfast, went to church, did some homework, read some books, and even had time to squeeze in a little movie at home. There were no big "ah-ha" moments (except for finding my son's lost shoes in the very back of the car). Nothing that occurred was overly deep or life-changing. Perhaps today was the same for you as well. In the Scriptures, life is compared to a race of endurance. There is a good reason for this metaphor. Most of us are in it for the long haul.

Day-to-day life can sometimes get a little "boring." Since 95 percent of our days are quite ordinary, it is time to up our game. Satan wants us to be comfortable in our daily routines. He wants us to become apathetic to the world around us. He wants us to get frustrated when dishes break, children disobey, cars stop working, and neighbors' yards grow to knee height. He wants to keep us in the mundane so he can distract us with little things and turn our songs of praise into anthems of complaints. Perhaps it is time we focus less on squeezing God into our schedules and instead let our schedules be saturated by God. In doing so, we might just see the hand of God more clearly in our day-to-day lives and even be a little more joyful!

In 1 Corinthians 10:31b, Paul challenges the church by saying, "…whatever you do, do it all for the glory of God." What does that mean? What does that look like? In this seven-week study, we will unpack numerous verses that will help us answer these questions. In the end, you will find that you have already been equipped with everything you need; and all you need to do is act.

My friend, my prayer for you is that in our time together, you will not just get into the Word, but let the Word get into you. We have good intentions, but it is time to stop simply opening books and start opening our hearts. God longs for you to be in the Word. You will become less like your old self and more like who Christ called you to be (2 Corinthians 5:17). That is how growth in Christ occurs. It does not matter where you have been. What matters is where you are going. Your past (no matter how much you might wish it could be changed) carefully helped to shape you into the woman of God that you are today and into the woman of God that you are to become.

God brought you into this study for a reason. Come and sit at His feet and learn from the One who is full of wisdom and abounds in love for you. God is behind you all the way. He is cheering for you when you need encouragement, catching you when you fall, and guiding you when you cannot find the way. My prayer for you is that no matter where you are on your walk, God will use this study to help deepen your relationship with Him. The more you learn about Him, the more you will want to know about Him. It is time to take it to the next level as we learn how to bring God the glory with what we have been given. Besides, it is much harder for Satan to pull the rug out from under your feet if you are already on your knees.

WEEK ONE

<hr/>

Quick to Listen: Recognizing Truth

Day One: Our Counselor (John 14:26)

Day Two: The Word of God (Hebrews 4:12)

Day Three: Quietly Waiting (Psalm 37:7)

Day Four: Your Good Shepherd (John 10:27–28)

Day Five: God's Workmanship (Ephesians 2:10)

Challenge Thought:

We are quick to accept something so miraculous as the death and resurrection of Christ but have a harder time wrapping our minds around a God who still actively wants to communicate with us. Do you find that this is true in your own life? This week we will be focusing on Scriptures that help remind us to anticipate and expect to hear truth as the Holy Spirit guides you using Scripture, prayer, godly counsel, and circumstances. We will look at how we are called to not only listen to the Word, but to live it out in our daily lives.

Our Counselor

"But the Counselor, the Holy Spirit, whom the Father will send
in My name, will teach you all things and will remind you of everything
I have said to you." —John 14:26

BEFORE WE DIVE INTO THE first lesson, please stop and take a moment to ask God to use the next few minutes of studying His Word to convict, challenge, and encourage you. If you are not used to doing this, use this study as a chance to try something new. It only takes a few minutes and you might be surprised by the results. Get in the habit of doing this each and every time you open His Word over the course of the next few weeks. Ask God to start opening the eyes of your heart (Ephesians 1:18). Try to avoid cutting corners and hurrying through questions just to get them done. A few honest and authentic answers are far more important than filling out an entire book halfheartedly. Pray that the Holy Spirit will help guide you and fill in the gaps as you learn more about Him.

In the next five days, we are simply going to focus on what Scripture says about how God directs our paths to bring Him glory. We will be looking at several Scriptures that shed some light on how God communicates with us through the Holy Spirit. Today's lesson is rich with information. It is important to review how God speaks truth into His followers in order to get the most out of your time in His Word. The application will come soon; just hang in there as we set the groundwork!

In the Old Testament, we read how God spoke *audibly* in a variety of different ways to a variety of different people. In the beginning of the New Testament, God broke the 400-year silence between Malachi and Matthew by sending His Son, Jesus, to the world. Jesus communicated truths about the Father to all who would listen. He had many conversations during His few decades on earth. He told parables and stories that would baffle and frustrate even the wisest of religious leaders.

After Christ's death and resurrection, there was another shift in how God mainly communicated with His followers. Shortly after Christ's ascension into heaven, God sent "His Helper," the Holy Spirit, into the world (Acts 2). There were a few examples of God speaking via other means from Matthew to Revelation, but today we will be focusing on several verses that tell how the Holy Spirit communicates with us and how He brings our requests to God.

> Before we dig into God's Word, take a few minutes to think about our loving God who chooses to communicate with us. Why do you suppose God would want to communicate to us? Do not just breeze over this one. Try to think of and list several reasons.

We serve a loving God (Jeremiah 31:3). He wants to rescue you from every evil attack (2 Timothy 4:18). He encourages you (Psalm 10:17). He comforts you (Psalm 34:18). He provides you with courage (Psalm 27:1). He wants to fill you with hope, joy, and peace (Romans 15:13). He wants to take all of your worries (1 Peter 5:7). He wants to give you wisdom (James 1:5). He wants to guide you and fulfill your needs (Isaiah 58:11). The list goes on and on. One of the reasons He chooses to communicate with us is for our own benefit.

We find the most information on the Holy Spirit, or "Counselor," in the New Testament. It is here that we will spend a majority of our time today as we unpack several of those Scriptures that give us a little more insight into the third person of the Trinity. In 1 Corinthians 2:11–12, we learn that the Holy Spirit is from God and knows His thoughts. In John 14:16, we see that He will be with us forever. In Romans 8:16, we find that the Holy Spirit lives inside believers.

Now that you know Who sent Him, how long He will be with us, and where He lives, let's look at what He does. Listed below are several passages that shed light on the tasks of the Holy Spirit. Look up each reference and take time to jot down some notes about what our Counselor does for believers. Pay close attention to those verbs. The first verse is particularly unique because it is Jesus (the Son) talking about God (the Father) sending the Holy Spirit—all of the Trinity in one little verse!

John 14:26

John 15:26–27

John 16:8, 13–14

Romans 8:26

Depending on what version of the Bible you have, you may have seen the Holy Spirit referenced as "the Friend," "the Advocate," "the Counselor," "the Spirit of Truth," or "the Comforter." The Holy Spirit teaches, reminds, testifies, convicts, guides, speaks, makes God known, brings glory to the Father, and intercedes for believers. He is unlike our sinful nature (Romans 8:4). Over the course of the next two days, we be taking a peek into how the Holy Spirit uses Scripture, prayer, godly people, and circumstances to "make God known to you" (John 16:15).

Day Two

The Word of God

"For the Word of God is living and active. Sharper than any double-edged sword, it penetrates even to dividing soul and spirit, joints and marrow; it judges the thoughts and attitudes of the heart."
—Hebrews 4:12

As we discovered in yesterday's lesson, God sent us the Holy Spirit after His Son left the earth. Before Jesus left His disciples, He told them that although He would not be with them in the flesh, He would not leave them as "orphans" (John 14:18). He loved them enough to not leave alone, so God sent them a "Counselor" to help them the rest of their days. Today we will be looking at the first of the four main ways God speaks to us today using the Holy Spirit as our guide—the Bible.

Begin by opening God's Word to "hear" what it has to say about itself. Please read 2 Timothy 3:16–17. What stands out to you in this verse?

Now look up Hebrews 4:12 and Ephesians 6:10–18 where we learn of the "Armor of God." The Word of God is compared to what piece of armor in these verses? Expound on what that analogy means.

Growing up, I was part of a Bible quizzing team. If you spent your childhood in the church, you, too, might have experienced something similar. "Sword Drills" also provided a unique opportunity to demonstrate one's ability to quickly locate a certain Scripture reference with sheer speed and agility. It became a competition to see who could look up verses the fastest. Now looking back, it was a cheesy game—but it served a huge purpose. God's Word plays an absolutely essential role in hearing God's voice. The more we are familiar with it, the easier it is to hear God. God's Word is meant to convict, challenge, and encourage. The Bible was never meant to sit on a shelf. If it sits there for too long, you might find yourself in a world of trouble.

As recounted in 2 Kings 22–23, King Josiah's workers stumbled across the Word of God during a huge renovation project of the temple. It had been neglected for quite some time. You do not need to read this entire account, but I want you to look at a few key verses.

When this dusty scroll was read, how did Josiah react (22:11)?

Why did he react that way (22:13b)?

What happened as a result of him hearing the Scripture read (23:1–3)?

Your Bible has probably not been buried under piles of rubble for years. It may, in fact, be getting a little dusty. You may not think it is a big deal now because all is going well; however, I want you take your eyes off the here and now and focus on the future. Over several months, what will happen if your Bible stays on the shelf? Pan out even further. What will happen to your children if they never see you modeling the importance of reading Scripture? What about your grandchildren?

Although the effects of not reading Scripture can have long term impacts on the generations to come, it most definitely effects our everyday lives as well. As you read earlier, the Word of God is alive and active.

What does 1 Thessalonians 5:21–22 challenge its readers to do?

We are to test everything. If we are to test everything, we need something against which to test it. We need our Guide, the Holy Spirit. We need our guidebook, the Bible. We have both! In tomorrow's lesson, we will be learning more about how God speaks to His followers using means other than the Scriptures, but there is something very important here that I do not want you to miss. No matter what you feel like God is calling you to do, He will never call you to do something that is contrary to Scripture. I cannot place enough emphasis on this. Our thoughts can deceive us. People (even godly individuals) can still mislead us. Even circumstances that "line up" can still "lead us into temptation" (Matthew 6:13). Just because it "feels right," does not mean we should proceed. That is why it is crucial that we spend time in the Word and meditate on it day and night. (Joshua 1:8).

Jesus participated in a little "Bible Quizzing" of His own. The enemy thought he had Jesus cornered until Jesus pulled out the Sword of the Spirit. (He memorized the Law at the Temple when He was just a boy). Check out the story in Matthew 4:1–11.

Jesus used a variety of Scriptures to avoid Satan's challenges. As you may have noticed, Jesus did not pull out written Word to cite these verses. Why is it so important to memorize Scripture?

You might consider memorizing Scripture a bit much to swallow. Fortunately, you do no need to eat it all in one setting. Just start with a bite. Then take another one. If you do not know where to start, a good place would be the "theme verse" listed at the top of the lesson each day. Take time to write the verse on a little notecard and place it somewhere where you spend time. Place one on the bathroom mirror, set one by the kitchen sink, tape one on the back of your phone, or hang up one in the office. Read them once or twice each time you see it. Rotate them through. Before you know it, your bites will turn into portions and your portions will turn into meals.

As Jesus was being tempted by Satan in the desert, He quoted an applicable verse from Deuteronomy 8:3b. It says, "…man does not live on bread alone but on every word that comes from the mouth of the Lord." It is time to start filling ourselves with God's Word—one bite at a time. When Satan comes to tempt us, we will not buckle under pressure. We will fight his lies with God's truth using the sword that has been placed in our hands.

Quietly Waiting

"Be still before the LORD and wait patiently for Him; do not fret when men succeed in their ways, when they carry out their wicked schemes." —Psalm 37:7

I N YESTERDAY'S LESSON, WE LEARNED how the Holy Spirit guides believers into God's truth through Scripture. The Word of God is active and still speaks to our hearts today with the help of our great Counselor. In this lesson, we will be looking at how God calls us to pray, seek godly counsel, and consider our circumstances to maintain a closer fellowship with Him.

Throughout Scripture we see a reoccurring theme of God communicating with mankind. From Adam and Eve in Genesis all the way to the end times in Revelation, the Word of God reveals a loving God who desires to be in fellowship with the faithful. The next several verses are ones that remind us that God desires for us to pray to Him.

Read 1 Thessalonians 5:16–18. How often are we to pray?

God wants us to be in constant fellowship with Him, not just before bedtime and meals. Have you ever thought about that? Prayer is not limited to certain times of the day. It can be anytime and anywhere. It can be sprinkled throughout your schedule. Prayer is the key into our hearts. If we start sending up little prayers of thanksgiving during the day, we may find our hearts becoming more and more appreciative of the little blessings God gives us each day.

> Please read Philippians 4:6 and record any thoughts below that might be helpful to you in your prayer time.

We are to be thankful for what we have, but we can send up our requests as well. Just as Abraham petitioned God on behalf of Sodom and Gomorrah (Genesis 18), God welcomes any requests. Sometimes we think that a request might be bothersome to God, but that is not the case.

Prayer can be healing as well. God calls us to cast our cares and worries on Him because He loves us (1 Peter 5:7). He wants us to learn from Him and take on His yolk because it is easy and light (Matthew 11:29–30). Our yolks are quite the opposite. They are heavy and burdensome. Most of the time I find the things that I worried most about were a total waste of time. Prayer can help remove the weight of our baggage and give it to God.

> 1 Kings 19:11–13 recounts a visit that the prophet Elijah had from God. Take a moment to read it and then record where Elijah heard God. Was it where you would expect?

> Now look up Psalm 37:7 and write it in the space below. Underline the two phrases that tell what Elijah had to do before He heard to voice of God.

We are to be still and wait patiently on God. I know that our busy lives leave little room for quiet reflection, but that might mean it is time to reprioritize. A.W. Tozer wrote: "It is important that we get still to wait on God. And it is best that we get alone, preferably with our Bible outspread before us. Then if we will we may draw near to God and begin to hear

Him speak to us in our hearts."[1] Elijah heard God in a gentle whisper, but he first needed to be silent to hear it.

The Israelites were pros at waiting. Were they good at waiting? Not really. We they impatient? Usually. That did not change the fact that they had to wait. They wandered through the dessert for 40 years before their children finally entered the Promised Land (Joshua 5:6). That is a lot of waiting! When you have to wait, God will renew your strength so you will not grow weary, but that does not mean it will be a walk in the park (Isaiah 40:31).

We need to constantly be in prayer. We are to be thankful and to share our requests with God. We are to be still and to wait patiently for a response. Rest assured that the Lord hears your requests (Psalm 5:3). He will be faithful to show you great things if you call out to Him (Jeremiah 33:3). Sometimes all we need to do is ask! His presence is near to all who call on Him in truth (Psalm 145:18). Take time to address any sin that might be holding you back (Proverbs 28:9). If you do not know what to pray, have no fear! The Holy Spirit knows you well and will intercede on your behalf (Romans 8:26). God is ready and waiting to hear what is on your heart.

We are to test everything against Scripture and pray, but sometimes it is nice to have words of advice from a godly friend. God describes the church as a body, with each person playing an important role to the health of the church. He never meant for us to live life alone. We are to live life together—which means we suffer together and rejoice together (1 Corinthians 12). We are better together. A stray sheep can be much more easily snatched by the enemy. The Father strategically places godly examples within the body. Seek them out for advice.

Look up Proverbs 12:15. How does this verse confirm the paragraph above?

Finally, God often speaks to us through our circumstances. You may be on the brink of a huge decision and do not know which way to turn. You may find yourself thrown into some horrible news and you do not know what your next step should be. There are no specific verses on what college to attend, who to marry (other than a believer), or whether or not you

---

[1]   Tozer, A.W. *The Best of A.W. Tozer.* Camp Hill, PA: Christina Publications, Inc, 1978, p. 25.

should adopt a child from overseas. Prayer and godly counsel play a huge role, but sometimes your path can still be unclear.

> Read Hosea 12:6 and record the three verbs in this verse that tell you what to do in the meantime.

We are to return to God, maintain love, and wait. If you have not heard a clear direction, perhaps the answer is "not yet" or keep waiting (Psalm 27:14). Remind yourself that God's timing is not our timing. His thoughts are not our thoughts, but He promises to accomplish what He desires (Isaiah 55:8–11). Commit your way to Him (Psalm 37:5). You can never be outside of the range of His guidance (Psalm 139:9–10). In Isaiah 30:21, the prophet Isaiah tells Israel that "whether you turn to the right or to the left, your ears will hear a voice behind you, saying, 'This is the way; walk in it.'"

You might find yourself in a place where you must make an immediate decision but feel like you have no clear guidance. Neither choice is contrary to Scripture. You have a clean conscious and no unresolved sin. You have been constantly praying for wisdom on what to decide. You have received godly counsel from a few sources and they all agree that either option is a good option. You have weighed the pros and cons of both scenarios. You have carefully considered how your decision will impact those closest to you. What should you do? Have you ever considered that perhaps God is allowing you to choose? Sometimes God gives us choices. Perhaps either situation can be used by Him in mighty ways, so His seeming "lack of response," might just be Him giving you space to choose. If you trust in the Lord and lean on Him, He will make sure that your paths are straight (Proverbs 3:5–6).

You have done a lot of work over the last three days. You have read several Scriptures and have been challenged to apply what you are learning to your own life. God has reminded you of truths that you maybe knew but had forgotten. Perhaps you were even convicted to rethink a certain aspect of your own life. Take time to jot down a few closing thoughts in the space below. Highlight a few things that you want to remember. Sometimes writing it down can be helpful. I have enjoyed studying God's Word alongside of you. Tomorrow we will be basking in the verses about Christ being our Good Shepherd and how His sheep hear His voice.

DAY FOUR

Your Good Shepherd

"My sheep listen to My voice; I know them, and they follow Me.
I shall give them eternal life, and they shall never perish; no one can snatch
them out of My hand." —John 10:27–28

ALTHOUGH I HAVE MINIMAL EXPERIENCE with sheep, I have heard a few stories about them before. I know they are cute and cuddly. You can feed them with bottles when they are young. Even though they are extremely loveable when they are little, they are not the same as they get older. Sheep are not very bright. In fact, they are quite dumb. They follow each other without giving it a second thought. They have been known to follow each other off the side of cliffs. They will wander off by themselves and get attacked by predators. The only redeeming quality of sheep (besides their wool) is that they can learn to recognize their shepherd's voice.

In the time of the Old and New Testaments, people were very well acquainted with sheep. We see shepherds and flocks appear throughout Scripture. David was a shepherd who was skilled at taking out large predators with only a slingshot, which came in handy when he fought Goliath. The angels appeared to the shepherds outside of Bethlehem announcing the Savior's arrival. Jesus often told stories and parables that tied directly to the world around Him. The story of the Good Shepherd, which you are about to read, was no exception. Today we are going to look more at how we are like sheep and Jesus is like the shepherd.

Please take a few minutes to briefly skim Jesus's words in John 10:1–30. His words were powerful enough that He was almost stoned by the Pharisees because they thought He was being blasphemous. What was He talking about in this Scripture?

There is so much to unpack in these verses. Let's break it down a little bit more. There are certain pieces that should not be overlooked that directly relate to hearing the voice of our Good Shepherd.

Jesus calls Himself "the Good Shepherd" repeatedly in this chapter. What does He say about His relationship with the sheep in verse 14?

Keeping in mind that Jesus's audience at the time was the Jewish people, why is verse 16 so important to us as non-Jewish (or Gentile) believers? (If you need an additional reference, Galatians 3:13–14 touches base on this topic as well).

How is our Good Shepherd different from all of the false ones who had come before Him (verses 8, 12, and 13)?

Now flip over to John 8:47 and then to Romans 8:9. These two verses pack a lot of punch! What do they both have in common? (Another way to recognize the Holy Spirit in believers is by the Fruit of the Spirit which we will cover in week four).

We are going to change it a bit to make it even more personal. Read John 10:27 at the top of the next page and fill in the blank with your name. Take a moment to ponder it and let it sink in. Reread it a few times out loud if necessary.

"_____ listens to My voice; I know her, and she follows Me."

The Good Shepherd knows you. He knows your flaws. He knows your shortcomings. Isaiah 53:6 reminds us that "we all, like sheep, have gone astray, each of us has turned to his own way; and the Lord has laid on Him the iniquity of us all." Even in the Old Testament we see snapshots of our Good Shepherd who would eventually lay His life down for His sheep. He knows how you are prone to wander. He still loves you. He rescues you from danger and every evil attack (2 Timothy 4:18). His love was so great that He laid down His life for His friends (John 15:13). He made us. We are the sheep in His pasture (Psalm 100:3). The grass is greener on *His* side. One day, the Good Shepherd will return to earth and divide the sheep from the goats (Matthew 25:31–48). Oh glorious day!

Once you start listening to the Good Shepherd by learning to hear His voice, you may find your own desires changing. You may want to focus on Him more. You may want to serve Him more. You may want to talk about Him more. You may actually find yourself hungry even after hearing a good sermon.

You have almost made it through the first week! If you find yourself struggling to apply what you are learning, stop and take a moment to ask God for His help.

In closing, please look up Psalm 95:7–8a and write it in the space below.

I challenge you to change the word "*if*" to "*when*." "Today, *when* you hear His voice, do not harden your hearts." Expect it. Anticipate it. Taste and see that the Lord is good (Psalm 34:8)!

DAY FIVE

God's Workmanship

"For we are God's workmanship, created in Christ Jesus to do good works,
which God prepared in advance for us to do." —Ephesians 2:10

GOD WANTS YOU NOT ONLY to enjoy what you have read but to apply what you have learned. He wants us to not only be touched but to be changed. He wants you to go deeper in your faith and to live it out your faith. Never stop seeking and growing!

Look up James 1:19–20a. What are we to be quick to do? What are we to be slow to do?

Peek ahead a few verses to James 1:22. Write this in the space below in your own words.

James is saying that we need to have less talk and more walk! When God speaks, people start moving. Think about Moses and the burning bush (Exodus 3). Although he hesitated at first, he eventually chose to obey and literally walked...and walked...and walked some more. Do not forget the Apostle Paul and his 180-degree turn from Christian-killer to gospel-spreader (Acts 9). Can you imagine how differently history would look if it were not Moses who led God's people from Egypt? Think about how many more believers from the early church would have perished under Saul's extreme persecution had he not been stopped. Saul would have never had his name changed to Paul. Think of the ministry Paul would have missed! The impact of people "doing" and not just "hearing" is extreme. Hearing the Word of God causes us to act.

Can you think any other examples in Scripture where God spoke and the recipient of His message responded?

We are to live out our faith. If you hear the voice of God but dismiss it as something else, have no fear, He will continue to remind you what He wants you to do. He will not allow you to forget what you have heard.

God is working all around you. He is still healing the sick, feeding the poor, loving the unlovable, and forgiving those who repent. He invites you to be a part of what He is doing in our generation.

Check out Ephesians 2:10. Write down what we were created to be and what God calls us to do?

As believers, we have all of God's resources at our disposal through the Holy Spirit. What a shame it would be if we never used them! How many of us do not shine our light? God calls us to be His workers, but it is hard to know what He wants us to do if we are not hearing from Him. Be open to His voice and take part in what God is doing all around you.

Sometimes (okay…often times) I try to be too smart for my own good. I try to rationalize God's tugging on my heart as something else. I try to explain it away or squish it into my own plan.

Have you experienced something similar, where God kept calling despite your ignorance? If so, please take a moment to share in the space below.

We serve a God who is actively working in us to bring Him glory (Philippians 2:13). Those who hear and obey will be blessed (Luke 11:28). There is an old hymn that you may be familiar with called "Trust and Obey."[2] The song lyrics are full of good theology. They do not say "trust and think about it" or "hear and weigh your options." God calls us to act! He does not *need* you to get involved, but He invites you to be a part of His work so that you can receive the blessing that comes from obedience.

> In closing, please record young Samuel's response to God found in 1 Samuel 3:10 that he spoke after an older, wiser God-follower confirmed that the voice he was hearing was from the Lord.

May Samuel's words be echoed in your heart as well as we close out this week.

[2]   Towner, Daniel Brink and John H. Sammis. *Trust and Obey*. 1887.

WEEK TWO

Oh, Be Careful Little Eyes: Focusing on Christ

Day One: Setting Your Priorities (Deuteronomy 4:29)

Day Two: Keeping Your Eyes on the Unseen (2 Corinthians 4:18)

Day Three: Finding True Satisfaction (1 Timothy 6:6)

Day Four: Maker of Heaven (Psalm 121:1–2)

Day Five: Eyes Wide Open (Psalm 119:18)

Challenge Thought:

What is your biggest priority in life? In other words, how do you spend most of your time? Where do you spend your money? What keeps you awake at night? We tend to put our life into "categories." We might go to school, head to work, or stay at home. We interact with family members, roommates, coworkers, and friends. Often times "church" and "God" have times carved out for them as well. Spending time with God each and every day is essential to growing in your faith. However, what would happen if we not only spent time alone with Him but also invited Him into each and every part of our day? God should never be limited to a two-hour weekly sermon or even just a thirty minute chunk of time each day. He should infiltrate your lifestyle—the places you go, the people you see, and the activities you do. Start thinking of some areas of your life that need God. Feel free to list them across this page.

DAY ONE

Setting Your Priorities

"But if from there you seek the LORD your God, you will find Him if you look for Him with all your heart and with all your soul." —Deuteronomy 4:29

Busy. Busy. Busy. All we are today is busy. We are running to doctor's appointments, work, the grocery store, dinner, a playdate, or even the kids' soccer practices. It is so easy in today's world to lose sight of our priorities.

Last week we learned the importance of simply taking time to "be still." Slowing down can help you to hear God better and deal with situations as they arise. Slowing down allows you to think through how you can serve your family that day. Slowing down helps give clarity to how you can help advance the kingdom of God with the people with whom you come into contact.

Look up Matthew 6:33 and write it in the space below. What happens when we seek God?

You might already be familiar with Jeremiah 29:11. Take a minute to read or reread it if necessary. Now look up the verses following the passage. Read verses 12–14 and record your thoughts below. When the exiles actively sought God, what did He promise would happen as a result?

Deuteronomy 4:29 (written out at the beginning of today's lesson) says that when you look with your whole heart, you will find Him. Have you prioritized your day so that you have time to seek God? "Looking" does not necessarily mean with your eyes. Although often times we can literally see the effects of God at work, it is also important that we seek Him with our hearts as well. We will be discussing this more in our fourth week of study.

The danger of "busyness" is that if we do not schedule time for God, we tend to move it down on our "to do" list. I am not saying that it has to be at a specific time of day (but for some of you that works the best), I am just saying to make sure you include it in your schedule. Know what time of day works best for you. If you have young children, I would suggest a time when the children are sleeping. If you are a morning person, what better way to start your day than with God? If you have children that are old enough to understand what you are doing and feel led to do so, invite them to sit with you during your quiet time and read their Bibles beside you. Discuss what you are learning. Only study late at night if you are a night owl; otherwise, you might find yourself starting to "nod off."

Check out the quote from *The Autobiography of George Muller* that warns of the potential dangers of not setting aside a time with God and how procrastination hinders your ability to enjoy the quiet time with your Savior.

> "You begin to work after only a few hurried moments for prayer. You leave your work in the evening and intend to read a little of the Word of God, but by then you are too worn out in body and mind to enjoy it. You often fall asleep while reading the Scriptures or while on your knees in prayer."[3]

I would strongly encourage you to do everything to the glory of God, as our theme verse says. Carving out time for God is great, but do not limit Him only to that time. If you are washing your dishes, thank God for providing for the physical needs of your family. If you are driving, thank God for the car that gets you from place to place. If you are tucking in your children at night, thank God for the precious gift of life that He has entrusted to you. Building your relationship with God is an ongoing process as your awareness of Him grows.

---

[3] Muller, George. *The Autobiography of George Muller.* New Kensington, PA: Whitaker House, 1984, p. 71.

Can you think of a chore that you perform at home daily? (It can be one that you enjoy or one that you dread). How can you praise or thank God during that time?

If He has not been your top priority, why are you waiting? Do not let your busyness "fill" you. You will only be left hungry and desiring more. He is quietly calling you into communion with Him. Stop and talk to Him right now. Tell Him what you are thinking.

If it has been awhile, and you feel like your relationship has slipped, have no fear. He is still there waiting for you with open arms. Do not let the enemy trick you into thinking that God is disappointed in you in any way. The opposite is true. Like the parable of the prodigal son (Luke 15:11–32), He is watching and waiting for you with open arms, ready to celebrate as soon as you come home. Seek first His kingdom (Matthew 6:33).

In closing, use the space below to write down any thoughts that come to you about what you learned today. If a certain Scripture stood out to you, if the Holy Spirit is lovingly convicting you of something you want to remember, or if there was a passage reference that you want to research further—write it down!

DAY TWO

Keeping Your Eyes on the Unseen

"So fix our eyes not on what is seen, but on what is unseen. For what is seen is temporary, but what is unseen is eternal." —2 Corinthians 4:18

YOU MAY HAVE READ THE title of today's lesson and wondered, "Is that even possible? How can one really keep her eyes on something she cannot see? What does that mean?"

Read 2 Corinthians 4:18 at the top of today's lesson. What does it mean to "fix our eyes?"

Each and every day, your eyes "see" hundreds of things. When the earth fades, so will those things (Matthew 24:35). Latest hairdos, speedy cars, money, designer clothes are temporary and will not last. Spiritual things, on the other hand, will last through all eternity.

What are some of these temporary things that cause you to struggle? Try to avoid flying through this question. Stop and think. Write it down in the margins. Add more to it tomorrow if something else comes to mind. It is time we acknowledge what distracts us, so we can own it and move on! Try to name at least three things that receive too much of your attention.

Now flip your attention from the things that you "see" to the "unseen" things you just read in 2 Corinthians 4:18. We are to fix our eyes on the unseen. What might these "unseen things" look like?

What might happen to us if we start focusing too much on the visible instead of the "unseen"?

Keep in mind that the visible includes not only material possessions but also mirrors, if you know what I mean. We scrutinize our appearance instead of appreciate God's creation. We desire what other people have and want it for ourselves. We worry about what others will think about us and water down the truth, which only hurts everyone involved. In each one of these scenarios, the object of our focus becomes ourselves and no longer the "unseen."

What kinds of things can we, as believers, do to keep our eyes fixed on the "unseen"?

Howard Hendricks, in his book *Living by the Book,* states that "Dusty Bibles lead to dirty lives. Either sin will keep you from this book or this book will keep you from sin."[4] It is crucial to stay in the Word, pray, fellowship with believers, accept correction when necessary, and serve. These are just the tip of the iceberg!

If you have been negligent in reading your Bible, God is inviting you to begin again. If you have guilt from not reading your Bible, remember that Satan loves to keep you in the dark hole of guilt and shame. Jesus encourages you to begin where you ended. On the second day of next week's study, we will look more into the difference between Satan's condemnation and the Holy Spirit's conviction. These are two very different things, and awareness of Satan's plan is the first step to getting out of his pit.

As far as Satan is concerned, you are wearing a giant target on your back. You are a sitting duck, and he is waiting to render you helpless. In our busy world about which we

---

4   Hendricks, Howard and William Hendricks. *Living by the Book.* Chicago: Moody Press, 1991, p. 9.

spoke yesterday, we learned that we need to prioritize and check to ensure that our most important things are not temporary.

We need to keep our focus on the One who is unseen. We need to keep our focus on the One who will never leave us nor forsake us (Deuteronomy 31:6; Hebrews 13:5). We need to keep our focus on the One who has loved us with an everlasting love (Jeremiah 31:3). In closing, read Titus 2:11–14 below.

> "For the grace of God has appeared that brings salvation to all people. It teaches us to say 'no' to ungodliness and worldly passions, and to live self-controlled, upright and godly lives in this present age, while we wait for the blessed hope—the glorious appearing of our great God and Savior, Jesus Christ, who gave Himself for us to redeem us from all wickedness and to purify for Himself a people that are His very own, eager to do what is good."

Think about what God has done for you. Think about what God is currently doing for you. Think about what God will do for you in the future. Although this verse is filled with rich application, focus on one truth. One day we will meet our Savior face to face, just as Zacchaeus did as he was sitting in a tree (Luke 19). Do not wait until you see Him to "fix your eyes upon Him." The opposite of the word "fixed" is "broken." Think about that for a minute as you close today's lesson. If they are not *fixed* on Him now, you are bound to be *broken*.

DAY THREE

Finding True Satisfaction

"But godliness with contentment is great gain." —1 Timothy 6:6

YESTERDAY WE LEARNED HOW TO set priorities and to "keep our eyes on the skies." Today we will be taming the "I want that" monster. We will be reminded of the importance of guarding our eyes so what we see does not take root in our hearts. We will confront the desires of our heart and realign them with Scripture.

Check out Matthew 6:22–23 and write it in your own words in the space below.

This brings a whole new meaning to the children's song "Oh, Be Careful Little Eyes,"[5] does it not? We have a Father looking down on us in love; and if we are to "fix our eyes on the unseen" and on Him, we cannot always be looking at others and coveting their earthly possessions. When it comes to what we are to value, we are to look *up* and not *out*.

---

[5] n.a. *Oh, Be Careful, Little Eyes, What You See*. Bible Truth Publishers. http://bibletruthpublishers.com/oh-be-careful-little-eyes-what-you-see/lets-sing-about-Jesus-67/lkh67LSAJ (accessed May 28, 2012).

I love Psalm 37:4. Take a minute to look up this frequently misinterpreted Scripture and write it in the space below.

What does this verse say we must first do in order to receive the desires of our heart?

This Scripture is often taken to mean that God will bless you with "stuff" if you delight yourself in Him. This verse means something quite different! If you truly delight yourself in Him, seek no personal advancement, and wish to only advance the kingdom of God on earth, do you really think that the "desires of your heart" will be more stuff? You will find yourself wanting quite the opposite. The desires of your heart will be toward the souls of others. You might be praying for a loved one to come to the Lord. You might be praying for boldness as you witness to a neighbor. You might be praying for supernatural strength as you speak in front of a group of people about the love of Jesus. You will find that your "desires" change more and more from requests that benefit you and those around you to petitions that advance the kingdom: Bibles given to new believers, clean water for those with none, and food handed out to the hungry. Philippians 4:19 says "…God will meet all your needs…" It says nothing about supplying your wants!

God wants to be the only desire of your heart. The Bible clearly teaches that He is a jealous God and that He does not deal kindly with those who worship "things" over Him (Exodus 20:4–5). He wants us to enjoy His love and be satisfied in Him alone. We are to worship the Creator and not His creation (Romans 1:25).

Please read 1 Timothy 6:6 at the beginning of today's lesson and fill in the blanks.

"Godliness with _____ is GREAT _____."

Contentment is such a simple word and concept, yet it is so difficult to obtain. Are you content, or do you find yourself trying to fill your emptiness with more things? Only God can fill that hole.

If you have been blessed with material possessions, praise God! Use it for His glory! If you have a golf membership, witness to the people there who think that they do not need God. Are you blessed with a beautiful home? Open your doors and invite others in. Do you have an extra car? Use it to bless a family whose car is being repaired.

Everything that you do, "do it all for the glory of God" (1 Corinthians 10:31b)!

Maker of Heaven

"I lift up my eyes to the hills—where does my help come from? My help comes from the LORD, the Maker of heaven and earth." —Psalm 121:1–2

WHEN YOU HAVE A PROBLEM, to whom do you look for assistance? Do you try to solve your own problems? Do you sometimes feel like God is too busy for you? Perhaps you feel like it is something you can control, so you attempt to manage it yourself to avoid "bothering" God. As we saw in week one, God longs for us to bring our requests to Him (Philippians 4:6). He also assures us that nothing is impossible for Him (Luke 1:37). Oftentimes if we try to handle the little things, they snowball into big things because they were not given to God in the first place.

Can you think of a time in your life when you tried to handle something on your own without giving it to God? How did that turn out?

Read Psalm 121:1–2 at the top of today's lesson. As you are reading, remember that this is a "song of ascents." It was a song that the people of Israel would sing on their way to the city of Jerusalem. They sang it to help them regain focus as they prepared their hearts for a time of great celebration. According to the song, where are we to fix our eyes?

From where does this Psalm state that our help comes?

Why do you suppose that the writer of the Psalm included that God is the Maker of heaven and earth? Does that make it easier or harder for you to cry out to Him?

Look up James 4:8 and write its first sentence below.

Once again we see the importance of keeping our eyes fixed on Jesus, the "author and finisher of our faith" (Hebrews 12:2).

There was a famous poem written in the 1930s called *Footprints in the Sand*.[6] In it, the author describes a dream. He dreamt that he and the Lord were walking along the beach. Looking back, he noticed two sets of footprints, but was surprised (and a little upset) that during the hardest times of his life, he noticed there was only one set of footprints. He felt like God had abandoned him. The Lord quickly brought light to the subject: The man, in fact, had not been walking alone as he presumed. It was during the tough times that God scooped him up and carried him. The one set of footprints belonged to the Lord and not to the man. What a powerful reminder of how God is near to us and even closer during times of great trial!

When it seems like God is a million miles away, it is time to remember the truth that God offers through His Word. When you cannot "see" Him, rest assured that He is right there beside you.

Psalm 34:18 echoes this truth. What does it say?

---

[6] Stevenson, Mary. *Footprints in the Sand.* 1939. http://www.footprints-inthe-sand.com/index.php?page=Poem/Poem.php (accessed May 28, 2012).

He is close to you when you are brokenhearted. He will never leave you (Hebrews 13:5b). God will draw near to you if you draw near to Him, just as He promised.

Read 1 John 3:1 to find out what else God is called. Write it in the space below.

He is our Father. He calls us His children. He, like any parent, knows when His children are crying. He even knows what their cries mean. He holds you when you are downhearted and carries you when you cannot walk. Nothing is impossible for Him (Luke 1:37). Do not try to carry it on your own. Instead, fix your gaze upon the heavens, to the One who gives help (Psalm 121:1). Give it to God!

Eyes Wide Open

"Open my eyes that I may see wonderful things in Your law."
—Psalm 119:18

PICTURE A TYPICAL HOUSEHOLD WITH small children on Christmas Eve. The children are way too excited to go to bed. Once they finally are in bed, they cannot sleep. Why? Anticipation. They know something big is about to happen. They are afraid that if they blink, they might miss something, so they keep their eyes wide open!

With our priorities in check and our eyes to the skies, we can now just sit and wait. God is moving all around you. You just need to be tuned in to see it. It is exciting! Sometimes I think I might miss something that He is doing around me, so I try not to blink.

Read Luke 24:13–35. Shortly after Christ's resurrection, He began appearing to people. The men in this passage were so concerned about their own circumstances and what was going on around them, that they almost missed what event?

The book of Isaiah prophesied of a day when the blind would see and the deaf would hear (Isaiah 35:5). The New Testament records several of these miracles that Jesus performed. Take a minute to look up John 9:1–12. Record what you "see."

According to John 9:32, why was this particular miracle such a big deal?

Jesus fulfilled Old Testament prophesies repeatedly. Although He healed the physical sight of the blind, He can also open our spiritual eyes as well.

Look up John 9:39–41. Record Jesus' words about spiritual blindness.

Open your eyes and ears to be aware of His invitation to join Him in His activity in this generation. When He speaks and you have confirmed that it is Him (as we discussed in our first week), do not try to reason it away. Listen and follow.

Look up Psalm 119:18. What is the psalmist asking God to do for him?

Check out Ephesians 3:20–21. What does this verse say God is capable of doing?

God is moving, and He is ready to use you (yes…you!) to help spread the Gospel and share His love with a fallen world. Are you ready? If you want to see how you can be His worker, He will show you in more ways than you can ask or imagine. Pull out your magnifying glass this week and look closely for opportunities to share Jesus with someone else. Do not blink or you just might miss something big!

Week Three

Think on Godly Things: Meditating on the Things Above

Day One: Living in the Past (Ephesians 4:22–24)

Day Two: Condemnation or Conviction (2 Corinthians 10:5b)

Day Three: Let Go and Let God (Matthew 6:34)

Day Four: The Daily Grind (Romans 12:2)

Day Five: Peace That Passes All Understanding (Isaiah 26:3)

Challenge Thought:

How often do you think about your past regrets? How often do you struggle with negative thoughts? How often do you worry about the uncertainty of the future? Your past, present, and future all play a crucial role as you mature in Christ. Your past is not a weight, but a stepping stool. The negative thoughts that are stuck in your brain need to be replaced constantly with godly thoughts. The future is not something that should cause anxiety, but should offer new ways for us to trust God. This week will look at how the Bible tells us we are to think in order to bring God glory.

Living in the Past

"You were taught, with regard to your former way of life, to put off your
old self, which is being corrupted by its deceitful desires; to be made new in the
attitude of your minds; and to put on the new self, created to be like God in true
righteousness and holiness." —Ephesians 4:22–24

THE BIBLE SAYS THAT "THERE is none righteous, no not one" (Romans 3:10). You
have sinned. I have sinned. We are all in need of a Savior. Satan is well aware of
our pasts. His goal is to keep us from the Father and to hold us back from living
the life that God desires for us to live.

How does Satan use the knowledge of your past to His advantage?

If you remember back to the first week, we learned about distinguishing truth from lies.
Satan uses your past to keep your eyes off the present. It also keeps your focus on yourself
and off God. Satan will try to seclude you and make you feel as if you are the only one who
has those thoughts. He will take truth and twist it just enough to deceive you. He is the
father of lies (John 8:44), and he wants nothing more than to render you ineffective in the
kingdom. Unfortunately, he is really good at what he does.

Please look up 2 Corinthians 10:5b and write it in the space below. (We will be revisiting this verse tomorrow.)

How does this verse apply in this situation?

Have you have ever experienced a time when Satan's voice tried to take your mind away from what God was calling you to do? Even if it seems small, please write a quick note about it in the space below.

If your thoughts are not lining up with Scripture, it is time to change your thinking. Satan is alive and well. "Be self-controlled and alert. Your enemy the devil prowls around like a roaring lion looking for someone to devour" (1 Peter 5:8).

How is scary is that picture? Satan is looking to make our weaknesses his strengths. If there is a stronghold in your life that he can grab, he will! If there is at least one thing in our past that either hurts, brings us shame, or makes us feel unloved, he will find it. It may feel huge. It may seem small. The fact is that all have sinned and fall short of the glory of God (Romans 3:23). We are sitting ducks with targets on our backs, so be on the lookout! Do not let Satan use your past as a way to bring you down.

Even David struggled with thoughts of the past. Read Psalm 25:7. What does David ask God to "forget?"

Our loving God knows that the struggle of the past is real. What does Isaiah 43:18–19 say we are to forget? What is God doing instead?

Paul echoed these truths in Ephesians 4:22–24. In these verses (listed at the top of our lesson), what distinguishes our old self from our new self?

Remember, God gave you the experiences of your past to help shape you into the woman you are today. It is not about where you have been; it is about where you are going.

Condemnation or Conviction

"…we take captive every thought to make it obedient to Christ."
—2 Corinthians 10:5b

YESTERDAY WE STUDIED HOW SATAN is the father of lies and how he uses our pasts to render us useless to the body of Christ. Nothing pleases him more than a lukewarm Christian (Revelation 3:16).

Please read John 8:1–11. Pay close attention to the last two verses. What does Jesus say to the woman caught in adultery?

Now read and record (in your own words) what is said in Romans 8:1.

This may be obvious, but just stay with me for a moment. If you are "in Christ Jesus," is it possible for you to be condemned?

If feelings of condemnation are not from Christ, who are they from?

Condemnation is a sinking hole. It is a sticky mess of lies that Satan weaves to keep you in a spot where you are an ineffective member of the body of believers. It is an unshakeable feeling of shame or guilt. What exactly does this mean?

Condemnation can come in many different shapes and sizes. It takes the focus off God and onto something (or someone) else. Condemnation might sound like, "You cannot host a dinner party for your new unbelieving neighbors to witness to them. You cannot cook, and your house is a mess." For some of you, thoughts of condemnation might say, "Your mother was a lousy mother. You will be, too. Why even bother?" Others might hear, "Why are you praying? God will not hear you after all of the 'stuff' you have in your past."

The next thing you know, you are home alone by yourself because you are too ashamed to have anyone over. You gave up teaching your children in the "way they should go" (Proverbs 22:6). You stopped praying because you were tricked into thinking it was meaningless. Your feet have been knocked out from underneath you. You are now a believer who is no longer walking, but lying face down on the concrete. Have you ever had one of those days/weeks/months/years?

> What kind of lies is the father of lies trying to say to you right now? (Remember that the things he says are contrary to Scripture and the fact that the Creator of the Universe is head over heels in love with you).

Conviction, on the other hand, is totally different. Conviction is not a place where one should feel "stuck" or "empty." It is an instrument or tool that God uses to keep His followers in the sheepfold and out of danger. Conviction is that still, small voice coaxing you to change your ways and come home. It is rooted in love and is meant for your well-being. It calls you to confess and repent. It calls you to let go and move forward. Sin is a heavy burden (Psalm 38:4). Conviction leads us into freedom as the weight of our mistakes are forgiven and removed (Psalm 103:12).

Review Jeremiah 29:11 once again. Now look up Romans 8:28. What do these verses say about God's plans for His people?

Now read John 16:8. In this passage, Jesus was speaking to the disciples about the Holy Spirit. What did Jesus say the Counselor would do upon His arrival?

Yesterday we read 2 Corinthians 10:5b. It says, "…we take captive every thought and make it obedient to Christ." What should you do if Satan comes knocking at your door?

Take those thoughts captive! Balance his negative ideas with the words of God in Scripture. Feeling afraid? "…God did not give us a spirit of timidity, but of power…" (1 Timothy 1:7). Feeling unloved? "…I have loved you with an everlasting love…" (Jeremiah 31:3a). Feeling overwhelmed? "Come to Me, all you who are weary and burdened, and I will give you rest… for I am gentle and humble in heart, and you will find rest for your souls. For My yoke is easy and My burden is light" (Matthew 11:28–30). Do not underestimate the power of Scripture. Post it in your homes. Keep verses in the forefront of your mind. Use your guidebook. The Bible was not written to be a decoration on a shelf.

In closing, look up Deuteronomy 11:18–20. Write this passage in your own words.

Let Go and Let God

"Therefore do not worry about tomorrow, for tomorrow will worry about itself. Each day has enough trouble of its own." —Matthew 6:34

TODAY WE WILL BE LOOKING at how Satan can also use the uncertainty of the future to cripple us like he uses our past experiences. The truth of the matter is (and you may have heard this said before) that we do not know what tomorrow holds, but we do know who holds tomorrow. One of my biggest mental struggles is not over the past, or the present, but the future. This lesson is one that I need to hear often—even multiple times a day!

Look up Matthew 6:25–34. If you are a worrier like me, you may want to read this passage more than once to let it "sink in." Then, write it in the space below in your own words.

What verse stands out to you the most in this passage?

Jesus said "do not worry." If we do something contrary to His command, we are sinning. By worrying about the future, you are not relying on God. We are buying into the lie that we ultimately have control. God has a big picture that we do not see. Sometimes, looking back, we can see how all things worked together for His glory. Sometimes, though, we will not know why something happened the way it did. We just have to trust and give God the reins.

> On a scale from 1 (go with the flow Joe) to 10 (droopy eyes because you cannot sleep at night because you are trying to solve the world's problems), where are you on the worry scale? Be honest!

> When trials come, do you really trust God, or do you make a backup plan (in case His plan does not work out)?

> You are not alone! When the writer of Psalm 94:18–19 had anxiety, what brought him joy? You may find it helpful to read this verse a second time.

> What does Proverbs 12:25 say about what anxiety does to our bodies?

> What should we do with all of the things that cause us to worry according to 1 Peter 5:7?

We should not live in the regrets of the past. We should not worry about the future. What are we supposed to do in the present? Tomorrow we will be focusing on this topic in greater depth. In the meantime, here is a verse to start your thinking.

Check out Colossians 3:2. Instead of setting your mind on earthly things, what should you do?

Does this remind you of anything that you learned last week? Your mind should be set on things above and your eyes should be to the skies. Let go of earthly things, and let God replace them. Our focus (mind and eyes) needs to remain on God at all times. How are you doing in this area? How can you improve it? If you need accountability, please feel free to share. If there is a need you have that can be met by your sisters in Christ—whether to pray for a big decision you have to make or to touch base with you occasionally to see how you are addressing an issue that you have with someone in your family, just ask! Use the space below to write any thoughts God is revealing to you at this time.

The Daily Grind

"Do not conform any longer to the pattern of this world, but be transformed by the renewing of your mind. Then you will be able to test and approve what God's will is—His good, pleasing and perfect will." —Romans 12:2

THE LAST THREE DAYS WE have covered two "don'ts" about which we should avoid focusing. The first was living in a past of regret. The second was living in the worry of an uncertain future. Instead, we are to focus on the things of above. Today we will focus on the present.

Now read Romans 12:2. How are we to avoid conforming to the world?

What do you think "the renewing of your mind" looks like?

How should you set about accomplishing this task?

The "renewing of your mind" is not a one-time event. It is ongoing. It needs to be repeated constantly. It is a discipline that must be practiced. *The Message's* translation of Psalm 1:2 says that you should "chew on Scripture day and night." I love the image this portrays. Oftentimes, we rush through meals and barely take the time to taste our food, much less chew it. Instead, I see a picture of a cow with all of the time in the world, quietly chewing... and chewing...and chewing. There is no end in sight. It is not rushed or crammed into a portion of the day but is a constant part of her everyday life. It is how we should renew our mind. It should be constant remembrance of Scripture sprinkled throughout the day.

Philippians 4:8 is an amazing verse that lays out specifically what "the things of above look like." It is a great place to start when learning how to filter your thoughts during the daily grind. Fill in the blanks below to complete the verse. (I used the NIV translation.)

"Finally, brothers, whatever is _____, whatever is

_____, whatever is _____, whatever is

_____, whatever is _____, whatever

is _____—if anything is _____ or

_____, THINK ABOUT SUCH THINGS."

I added a little emphasis to make a point. What about you? Think about a time during the day when you struggle to keep your thoughts positive. It might be first thing in the morning when you are overwhelmed trying to get yourself ready and out of the door. It might be mid-day when you are trying to catch up on your chores around the house. You may find yourself fighting negative thoughts more during the evening when you realize that you have accomplished almost nothing that day and are totally exhausted. Recognize patterns of negativity to avoid ruts and be on the lookout.

Now think of a way that you can change those negative thoughts to something that is positive and falls under the principles taught in Philippians 4:8. Brainstorm any ideas below. (Keep this verse at hand because it will come up again momentarily.)

When negativity arises in the future (perhaps even later today), challenge your thoughts and align them with Scripture. It may seem silly at first, but keep at it! Allow the Holy Spirit to reveal to you areas on which you need some work. He will show you (in a convicting, non-condemning way). Then, keep practicing to take those thoughts captive.

> Do you have a story to share about a time where you took captive your negative thoughts and started to think about the things above? Celebrate this victory and think back to it when you are feeling discouraged.

> Often times we stop at verse 8 when we read this passage, but I want you to keep reading into the next verse. What will God do as a result?

> What do Paul and Timothy challenge the church in Philippi to do in verse 9?

If we put what we have learned into practice, we will have the peace of God. This is where we will stop in our time together today because it is a great transition into our next lesson. Tomorrow we will be studying this peace—the peace that passes our human understanding. Even though you are done with this lesson, continue to let the Holy Spirit teach you throughout the day as He brings what you have been studying to mind. Be on guard for Satan's lies as you continue to guard your thoughts.

Peace that Passes All Understanding

"You will keep him in perfect peace him whose mind is steadfast,
because he trust in You." —Isaiah 26:3

HOW MANY TIMES IS THE word "peace" used throughout the Bible? Care to take a guess? The word "peace" is 249 times in the New International Version (and even more often in other versions). Now that is a lot of peace![7]

Isaiah 26:3 is written at the top of the lesson. Take a few seconds to read it if you have not already taken the time to do so. I am not much of a math guru, but see if you can help me solve this equation using the words in the verse.

_____ mind + _____ in God = perfect _____

What does a steadfast mind look like?

---

[7] Bible Gateway: A Division of Zondervan Publishing. https://www.biblegateway.com/quicksearch/?quicksearch=peace&qs_version=NIV (accessed on April 9, 2016).

What does it mean to trust in God?

What does God promise He will do for us in this verse?

Is it possible for you put your trust in other things? Think of a few examples (such as *people, money,* or *material possessions*) and think of the consequences of putting your trust in these things.

Now read Isaiah 40:28–31. What are a few key points to this passage?

Earlier this week we discussed how Satan's lies can cause us to stumble instead of walk. We will also be addressing the topic of running with perseverance in a later week. I love how Scripture just ties everything up loose ends, don't you?

In Romans 8:5–9, Paul describes the difference between those that live according to the flesh and those that live according to the spirit. In the space below, write out the differences between the two types of people.

Go back and reread the characteristics of those that live by the Spirit. *Circle the two words* that describe the mind. (If you neglected to add them, do it now.)

Did you see them? They were "life" and "peace." Those words seem so contrary to the dying world around us. The world tells us that living by our own desires gives life. However, as believers, we know that we are not really alive until we have died to ourselves and our sinful desires (Romans 6:11).

Thank you for your faithfulness in doing this week's study. Today's lesson was short and sweet but hopefully challenged you to consider where you are placing your trust. Keep pursuing a deeper relationship with God! Allow Him to come, to convict, and to change you. Focus your thoughts on Him and His truths—not on the lies and distractions around you. Avoid the weight of the past and the worries of the future. Do not grow weary. Instead, soar like an eagle in the present. Next week we will turn our focus from our minds to our hearts.

> Take a moment to reflect on the five lessons we covered this week. Feel free to skim the pages. What stood out to you that you want to remember? Write any thoughts in the space below.

WEEK FOUR

A Healthy Heart: Loving as Christ Loved

Day One: All About Love (Galatians 5:22–23a)

Day Two: Our First Love (1 John 4:10)

Day Three: Taking Last Place (Matthew 20:16)

Day Four: Welcome Home (Isaiah 1:18b)

Day Five: A Cheerful Face (Nehemiah 8:10b)

Challenge Thought:

Jesus taught that it is not the healthy who need a physician but the sick (Matthew 9:12). What do you think He meant by this statement? Do you think your heart is "healthy?" Why or why not? In our lessons this week, we will discover how a healthy heart displays God's love to His hurting world; but we must first look at what authentic love is.

DAY ONE

_____

All About Love

"But the fruit of the Spirit is love, joy, peace, patience, kindness, goodness, faithfulness, gentleness, and self-control." —Galatians 5:22–23a

THIS WEEK WE ARE GOING to be learning/reviewing what you already know about love. First, we are going to do a little review about what love is by going to the chapter in the Bible commonly referred to as the "Love Chapter." Please look up 1 Corinthians 13:4–8a (NIV) and use it to fill in the blanks below.

"Love is _____, love is _____. It does

not _____, it does not _____, it is

not _____. It is not _____, it is not easily

_____-_____, it is not easily _____,

it keeps no record of _____. Love does not _____

in evil but rejoices with the _____. It always _____,

always _____, always _____, always

_____. Love never _____."

Before we go any further, I want to clarify something. From the time we were little, the world has instilled in us an improper view of love. We have learned that love is based on emotion. It tells us that love is a feeling much like a princess experiences in a fairy tale. Real love is something quite different. It is a choice we make. It often comes with strong feelings, but true love is making the decision to pursue a relationship. Love is no easy task. If it were, there would be no need for 1 Corinthians 13. We need constant reminders of how to love as God calls us to love. I am not simply referring to loving a spouse. Sometimes it is difficult to love a neighbor, our children, a friend, or a coworker.

> Can you think of a time in your life when you felt a call that had to be from God to love someone?

As a believer in Christ, you have been given the Holy Spirit to be your guide through life (as we saw in week one). One of the ways that you can tell the Holy Spirit is in you is the presence of His fruit. You will find yourself practicing the virtues that have been frequently called the "Fruit of the Spirit." The list of these "fruits" can be found in Galatians 5:22–23a (ESV) as written below.

> "But the fruit of the Spirit is love, joy, peace, patience, kindness, goodness, faithfulness, gentleness, self-control."

Please back and underline each of the nine fruits. What was the very first fruit on the list? *Go back and circle it.*

In review, we know what love looks like. We know that, as believers, we have the ability, through Christ, to love. In the next few days, we will be looking at our Savior as the ultimate example of love, the reasons why we should love, who we should love, and the importance of having a healthy heart so we can love.

> Before we end today's lesson, flip to Colossians 3:12–14 and read the verses. Write what you read in your own words below.

Why do you suppose Paul, the author of Colossians, separated "love" from the other fruit here?

Throughout the Bible, you will see that God's love is the thread with which the rug of Scriptures was woven. One cannot read the Scriptures without the love of God making its way into every story, parable, and event that took place in history. 1 John 4:16 states that "God is love."

In closing, go back and read 1 Corinthians 13 at the beginning of the lesson. Wherever you see the word "love," write "God" above it. I challenge you to reread it out loud, so you are not only seeing it, but hearing it as well.

God is the ultimate picture of what love looks like. Tomorrow we will be looking closer at His unfathomable love.

DAY TWO

Our First Love

"This is love: not that we loved God, but that He loved us and sent His one
and only Son into the world that we might live through Him." —1 John 4:10

MORE THAN LIKELY, IF YOU grew up in church, you are familiar with John 3:16 where it talks about God's love for the world. Have you ever read John 3:16 and taken it personally?

"God so loved _____ (*insert your name*) that He gave His one
and only Son, that whoever believes in Him shall not perish but have eternal life."

That statement sure packs a lot of punch. It is the whole Gospel message packaged up into one tidy little verse. That sure is a lot of love!

Look up 1 John 4:10 and write it in the space below.

Now read John 15:13 and write it below.

What in these two verses seems to be the ultimate demonstration of love?

This same God, who sent His only Son to take the punishment for your sins so you would not suffer eternal separation from Him, loves each part of you. Christ suffered through a painful love story for a fallen world that rejected Him. His desire to have a personal relationship with us is what separates Christianity from other religions. If God loves the world that much, it might just be time that you and I start loving others, too.

From pulpits all around the world, you will hear that salvation is a "free gift." It is true to some extent. Salvation is free for you. It is free for me. However, it came with a heavy price tag for Jesus. We must never forget that, although salvation is a freely-offered gift, it cost Christ everything.

Take a moment to look up the following sets of verses. Then complete the sentences beside each reference.

1 John 4:19: We love because …

John 14:23; 1 John 5:3: Those who love God will…

God knew you before you were ever conceived (Jeremiah 1:5; Psalm 139:13). He has loved you with an everlasting love (Jeremiah 31:3). His sacrifice on the cross was the ultimate depiction of love (John 15:13). He can love you like no one else. His love is not earthly. It is not based on what you can do for Him. It is a gift that has no strings attached (Ephesians 2:8–9). He was your first love and He wants to be your only true love (Revelation 2:4). It is pretty hard to not love the One who loves you that much!

DAY THREE

Taking Last Place

"So the last will be first, and the first will be last." —Matthew 20:16

WE LIVE IN A SOCIETY that has taught us that we have rights. We get a vote. We get to choose what or who we think is best for us. We deserve to live a better life. God's society does not work that way. Today we are going to spend quite a bit of time diving into Scripture together to see what God has to say about the subject of entitlement.

Matthew 20:16 sums up the "hierarchy" of God's Kingdom. What does this verse say?

Sooner or later, what is in our hearts is going to come out. There has to be a delicate balance of humility and confidence. You do not want to be proud, but you also do not want to have low self-esteem. Studying Scripture and obeying Christ will help you learn more about who you are in Him and who He calls you to be. As human beings, we do not have the ability to possess any sort of balance without Him.

The Bible clearly states whom we are to love. There are several of them here, but I encourage you to take the time to read them and write down anything that speaks to you.

Matthew 5:44

Matthew 22:37

John 13:34

Philippians 2:3–4

The Bible clearly teaches that we, as believers, are to love God and to love our neighbors—including our enemies (Mark 12:30–31; Matthew 5:43–48). In each one of these verses, someone that you know well is almost completely overlooked. Can you think of who this might be?

It is you! The Scripture very rarely reminds us to take care of ourselves. We already do that. In fact, often times we do that a little too well! Instead, it encourages us to do the opposite of what the world does. We are to serve others, just as Christ served others while He was on earth. This is what sets followers of Christ apart from the world.

I have heard it said that "the only way up is down." As we read today, it is the first who will be last and the last will be first (Matthew 20:16). We must learn to be a servant of all (Mark 9:35). We will be learning more about being a servant in a few weeks; but until then, practice loving others. As I often sang in church as a little girl, "They'll know we are Christians by our love."[8] That means sometimes we are going to be called to take last place.

---

8   Arends, Carolyn. *They'll Know We are Christians By Our Love*. Los Angeles: F.E.L. Publications, 1966.

Day Four

Welcome Home

"Though your sins are like scarlet, they shall be as white as snow; though they are red as crimson, they shall be like wool." —Isaiah 1:18b

THERE IS A SONG BY Shaun Groves entitled "Welcome Home."[9] The lyrics describe the imperfect heart that God seeks to call His home.

Our hearts are filled with guilt, shame, and greed. We hide our clutter and our dust, yet still God is there, knocking and waiting. If our hearts are filled with all of this "mess," is there any room for love? My guess is no.

Matthew 12:34b warns of the danger of having a "bad" heart. The verse says that "...out of the overflow of the heart the mouth speaks." Not only is your heart bad, so are the words out of your mouth (more to come next week). It sounds like a downhill run from there. In order to do everything for the glory of God, you need to guard your heart.

With an unhealthy heart, you will make unhealthy decisions. *Pilgrim's Progress* refers to the soul being "cleansed of sin, making it more hospitable for the King of Glory."[10]

Look up 1 John 1:9. What does this verse say we must do to be forgiven and cleansed from all sin?

---

9   Groves, Shaun. "Welcome Home." *Invitation to Eavesdrop.* Nashville, Tennessee: Rocketown Records, 2001.

10   Bunyan, John. *Pilgrim's Progress.* Chicago: Moody Press, 1964, p. 32.

Please reread Isaiah 1:18b at the top of today's lesson. What two "white" objects are used in this metaphor?

If you have prayed to receive Christ as your Savior, He has made you white as snow. Do not start trying to bring filth back into your heart. If you have already done so, do not let Satan's lies condemn you. Instead, it is time to repent and let God do a little house cleaning!

1 Peter 2:11 has something to say about this. What does Peter tell believers in Christ to abstain from doing and why?

Now read the next verse—verse 12. Why is abstaining from sin so important?

I love this! If we abstain, others will see and give glory to God. Let everything you do be to His glory. If we, as pilgrims, fall into the snare of sin, we will be too busy at war with our own self to be fighting the real war. That is why Peter urges us to guard our hearts from sin. If we do not guard our hearts, we are inviting Satan to hold us captive. Instead, invite Christ over and let Him decorate. He is much better.

In the world of real estate, there is a two-word phrase that packs a whole lot of punch—"curb appeal." If a house looks crummy on the outside, the assumption is true of the inside. God does not look at us with a "curb appeal" mentality.

Read 1 Samuel 16:7 and record the difference between how the Lord sees and how man see the heart.

In the verse, God is telling Samuel not to focus on David's outward appearance. As we have heard from a young age, "it is what's on the inside that counts."

You might look like you have it all together right now, but what about your "insides?" Have you spend as much time decorating your heart as you spend each morning on your "curb appeal?" What parts of your life need light and decluttering? Think through each one of this questions. Write any thoughts that come to mind in the space below.

God already knows what is in there, yet He stands knocking at your heart's door, waiting for you to let Him inside (Revelation 3:20).

Write out John 14:23.

Go back and underline the words *love* and *obey* on this page (or whatever similes your translation uses). Now draw a little house around the word "home" or "abode."

Too often pride stands in our way. Pride builds up walls inside of us. Although sin might seem like a good idea at the time, it only puts another barrier between you and God (and often times your loved ones). As more walls go up, you will find that your heart gets darker and darker. It is a slow fade. However, nothing (even a bunch of walls) can separate us from Christ's love (Romans 8:38–39). He is ready to reclaim your heart, remove its walls, and repurpose your life—and all you have to do is ask.

Write out an invitation in the space below asking Christ to decorate your heart. Make it simple or as fancy as you wish. List any places that might need a little extra attention to detail. I realize that this might be out of your comfort zone, but give it a shot (and maybe have a little fun in the process).

A Cheerful Face

"...the joy of the LORD is your strength." —Nehemiah 8:10b

I N THE FIRST LESSON THIS week, we briefly read about the "Fruit of the Spirit." The first one was love. Today we are going to address the second one—joy! Hopefully just reading that word brings a smile to your face. Proverbs 15:13 says that "a happy heart makes the face cheerful." The health of heart directly impacts your face. When was the last time you smiled?

A few years ago, my Bible study leader challenged the ladies in our group to intentionally place themselves around joyful people. They just might positively impact you. There is nothing more contagious than joy!

Do you have a Christian friend that is a joy to be around? What makes her so joyful?

Look up 1 Thessalonians 5:16 and Philippians 4:4. How often are we to be joyful?

Think about yourself for a moment and a time that you felt great joy. Write it down and try to pinpoint what made it so joyful.

I am guessing that whatever you wrote down was a blessing of some sort. It was possibly the addition on of a new family member, the purchase of a new home, a wedding date, the salvation of a loved one, or the answer of a long-time prayer request.

What if someone wrote down a time of great suffering or a trial? Have you thought about that? I have seen grieving widows who proclaim the name of the Lord. I have seen people lose their jobs and praise God, knowing that He has a plan for their lives. I have seen marriages crumble and the one left standing in the dust stepping out in faith and trusting God. How is this possible? Praising God during the storms of life? Joy during tribulation? What is that all about?

You may already know this verse in Nehemiah 8:10b. If not, take a minute to look it up and fill in the blank below.

"The _____ of the LORD is your strength."

Can we still have joy even during the tough times? Absolutely. The world will gaze in wonder because it is against everything that they know. God can use the most horrible circumstances to point people to Him.

James 1:2–3 echoes the idea of joy during difficult situations. What does this passage suggest should be the reason for our joy?

What is the cause of joy in Acts 2:26–28?

What gives David joy in Psalm 16:11?

What makes the writer of Psalm 92:4 sing for joy?

We have plenty of reasons to be joyful— faith that builds with trials, eternal life with Christ, God's presence, and His awesome works. Read 1 Peter 1:8–9 below. *Underline or highlight any words that stand out* to you as you are reading.

"Though you have not seen Him, you love Him; and even though you do not see Him now, you believe in Him and are filled with an inexpressible and glorious joy, for you are receiving the goal of your faith, the salvation of your souls."

We have a thousand more reasons to be joyful! As you end today's lesson, write down 20 mores "blessings" or things for which you can be thankful. When you struggle with negative thoughts during the day, think back to this list and give thanks.

WEEK FIVE

***

Taming the Tongue: Glorifying God with Your Words

Day One: Praising and Pleasing God (Matthew 12:34b)

Day Two: Let Your Words Be Few (Ecclesiastes 5:2)

Day Three: Keeping Your Words in Check (James 1:26)

Day Four: Building Up Others (Hebrews 10:24)

Day Five: Created to Glorify (Psalm 63:3–4)

Challenge Thought:

Women speak, on average, roughly 16,000 words per day.[11] What percentage of your daily speech is devoted to build up others? How much is used to praise God? How much is devoted to give correction? Does gossip ever creep into your speech? What about unkind words? How often do you apologize? (If you are like me, I am certain that a small percentage of daily words is simply repetition of something spoken earlier that was "tuned out" by the intended recipient). This week, we will learn the importance of taming our tongues in order to bring glory to the Father.

---

[11] Phillips, Ashley. "Study: Women Don't Talk More Than Men." *abcNews*, July 5, 2007, http://abcnews.go.com/Technology/story?id=3348076&page=1 (accessed May 28, 2012).

Praising and Pleasing God

"For out of the overflow of the heart the mouth speaks." —Matthew 12:34b

L AST WEEK WE TOOK SOME time studying what God's Word says about our hearts. This week we are transitioning from the heart to the mouth; but before we get into today's lesson, let's review Matthew 12:34b (NIV) and fill in the blanks below.

"For out of the overflow of the _____ the _____ speaks."

Now read James 3:8–12 and sum it up in the space below.

Ladies, if you have an issue with the words that come from your mouth, you must first get to the root of the problem…your heart! That is why we looked into our hearts before addressing the topic of our mouths. The mouth cannot be kept under control without our hearts being in check first. Hopefully, last week gave you some insight into how this can be done.

Now, let's take a look at how the heart and tongue unite through the aspect of worship. David, "the man after God's own heart" (Acts 13:22), wrote the lyrics of Psalm 19. The chapter begins with him writing about the heavens declaring God's glory. Verse 14 is a prayer to God.

> What does this verse say about the words of his mouth and the meditations of his heart?

If it is not pleasing, what good is it? Let me ask it a different way—do you mean what you sing? When you are singing at church, do you really think about what you are singing, or do you just sing? If you mean it, you are worshipping. If you are not meditating as you sing, you are just making noise. Now let me ask that first question again. If it is not pleasing, what good is it?

> Look up Psalm 40:3 and read it twice. Let these words simmer. According to this verse, who is it that puts a song in our mouths?

> Why did He put the song in your mouth?

He desires our praise! If we cease to praise Him, even the rocks will cry out (Luke 19:40)! Our mouths were meant for praise. In heaven, I have a feeling we will be using our mouths to sing a lot of praises. Why wait?

Next week we will be looking into our "hands" and how they are to be used to serve others. In our final week together, we will be looking more into our "feet" or the sharing of our faith. How does this all tie together? At the beginning of today's lesson, we reviewed how the heart affects our mouths. How do our mouths affect our feet? How do our mouths affect our hands? The beautiful thing about studying all of the parts of the body at once is that we can see (as we saw today) how they all tie together. If our lips are truly praising, our hands and feet should be moving as well. In other words, we should be living out our faith if we mean what we are singing.

Now let's turn the tables. It is true that we are to sing about our awesome Creator, but have you ever stopped to think that maybe He sings over you, too?

Check out Zephaniah 3:17. This verse is referring to the future of Jerusalem. What does this verse say gives God delight?

How does He quiet His people?

What does the last portion of this verse say about how He rejoices over His people?

Is there anything that God is telling you to do after today's lesson? If so, write it in the space below.

Let Your Words Be Few

"Do not be quick with your mouth, do not be hasty in your heart to utter anything before God. God is in heaven and you are on earth, so let your words be few." —Ecclesiastes 5:2

MOMS ARE AWESOME MULTI-TASKERS. THEY can talk on the phone, write a check to pay the electric bill, stop a quarrel from starting, and make breakfast all at the same time. Even though they can do all of these things simultaneously, have you ever noticed how hard it is for them to talk to someone while they are listening to someone else? Maybe you have experienced this as well. Think back to high school (for some of us that is a little foggier than for others) when you were talking to a friend beside you when you should have been listening to your teacher. Did you really hear what the teacher was saying while you were talking? It is not an easy task.

In our first week of study, we learned more about the importance of being still before God. Why is this so important?

If you are listening, how much can you really say? If we are "tuned into" the Creator of the universe, we might find ourselves talking less and listening more.

Solomon, the wisest man ever to live (1 Kings 4:29–31), had a few things to say about our words when we are in God's presence.

Read Ecclesiastes 5:1–7 and record any thoughts that arise below.

Matthew Henry challenges believers to approach God's house with humility and reverence, recognizing who we are not and who He is. He says, "Religious exercises are not vain things; but, if we mismanage them, they become vain to us."[12] When you go to church, what is your mindset? Has it become just a routine to you? Is it a "to do" that needs a check beside it before you can proceed with the rest of your week?

Henry goes on to address that the words of our mouths are a byproduct of our hearts. We must carefully think through our words before we speak them. "Thoughts are words to God, and words are but wind if they be not copied from the thoughts."[13] He calls this separation of words and thoughts "lip-labour." If we forget to think first, our mouths are doing all the work. Do we really want to be women who do not choose our words carefully? Maybe our moms were right after all when they used to tell us to "think before we speak."

In Proverbs 10:19 (NIV), Solomon had more to say about the mouth. Please turn to that passage now and, after reading it, fill in the blanks to complete the proverb.

"When _____ are _____,

sin is not absent, but he who _____ his

_____ is _____."

Can you think of a time when your mouth has gotten you into some trouble? I will not have you write this one down, but I am almost certain that you can think a time or two when your words created a problem for yourself and probably others as well.

---

[12]   Henry, Matthew. *Commentary Volume 3: Job to Song of Solomon*. New York: Fleming H. Revell, n.d., p. 1006.

[13]   Ibid.

In the New Testament, James echoes the teachings of Solomon. In James 1:19–20, what does he encourage us to do?

According to verse 20, why is this so important?

Check out Matthew 12:36. For what will we all be held accountable on judgement day?

I do not know about you, but whenever I hear something repeated (whether in everyday life or in the Scriptures), my ears perk up. We have all experienced a time in our lives when our mouths got us in trouble and we wound up hurting someone else when it was not necessarily our intention. Then, we must begin the seemingly long process of seeking forgiveness from the person we offended. Let's try harder to guard our mouths in the first place. Let your words be few. Think before you speak. We will continue with this thought in tomorrow's lesson. Well done!

Keeping Your Words in Check

"If anyone considers himself religious and yet does not keep a tight rein on his tongue, he deceives himself and his religion is worthless." —James 1:26

LET ME START THIS WEEK by saying that I am proud of you for your perseverance with this study! My hope and prayer for you all is that you are being encouraged daily. I pray that, even though some of these verses may be familiar, that God would use His Word to teach you something new and to convict you (and not condemn you) to become the woman of God that He desires for you to be.

As a first grade teacher, we were always encouraged to word our classroom rules in a positive manner. Instead of "Don't run" we were to say "Walk please." Instead of "No talking in the halls," we were to encourage students to "Be respectful of other students' learning time." Everything was light and fluffy. There is a time and a place for that. Tomorrow we will be looking more into the "dos" of speaking, but first we must knock down some of the "don'ts." You have a tough road in front of you, but you can do it!

James, the brother of Jesus, grew up in a Jewish home. Even though he became a follower of Jesus after Jesus' resurrection, James still held on to his strong Jewish heritage. As a result, he was able to convert many Jewish people to Christianity. If James had something to say, he said it fearlessly. He did not water Christ's teachings down, even if it meant stepping on some toes. Sometimes I wonder if he felt the need to make up for lost time.

Look up James 1:26. What does this eye-opening verse say about "religious people" who do not keep a tight rein on their tongue?

It seems harsh, but you really cannot be an effective part of God's team if you are useless. James challenges us to guard our tongues. From what types of things must we guard them from? Check out the verses below and write your thoughts. If you know of any other verses, please feel free to write them in the margin. As you write, *underline any of the areas on which you would like to work* in your own life.

Proverbs 12:22

Proverbs 13:3

Proverbs 26:28

Colossians 3:8

I Peter 3:10

Now look up James 3:8. What does verse this say about the tongue?

Beware! You in your own strength will never be able to control your tongue. We need to rely on God to help out with the taming process, a process which He begins in our hearts.

Matthew 15:8 quotes the words of Jesus referring to the Pharisees. He says, "These people honor Me with their lips, but their hearts are far from Me." May our hearts follow Jesus and my His words be the ones that our spoken from our lips. In closing, read the prayer below that David recorded in Psalm 141:3–4.

"Set a guard over my mouth, O LORD;
Keep watch over the door of my lips.
Let not my heart be drawn to what is evil,
To take part in wicked deeds with men who are evildoers;
Let me not eat of their delicacies."

Amen!

DAY FOUR

Building Up Others

"And let us consider how we may spur one another on toward
love and good deeds." —Hebrews 10:24

WE NEED TO MAKE SEVERAL deposits in someone's life before we are able to make a withdrawal. Correction is easier to take if you know the intentions of the person who is offering you guidance. Today's lesson will focus on how we, as believers, can bring glory to God by depositing words of encouragement into the lives of others.

Have you ever been corrected/guided by another believer? Briefly describe your experience, including your initial reaction and your response.

Sometimes correction is not easy to hear. David had a different perspective. Check out what he has to say about the subject in Psalm 141:5 and write a brief summary below.

Proverbs 10:11a says, "The mouth of the righteous is a fountain of life." How can we be a fountain of life that encourages others?

Let's look at Scripture and see what it has to say about the words from a righteous mouth. Please *draw a heart* by any of the references that also reference the heart.

Proverbs 10:31

Proverbs 16:23

Proverbs 22:11

Colossians 4:6

As I was cleaning up after a birthday party for my son, I realized just how much easier it is to tear down than to build up. The same is true with our words! All it takes is a matter of seconds to tear down a relationship in which you have invested years. Let's turn our focus toward building each other in wisdom, instruction, grace, and (not to mention), love.

Look up Hebrews 10:24–25. What is one way you could "spur" on someone else?

Why should believers meet together on a regular basis?

What are the two things that "spurring" initiates?

I love the enthusiasm that the word "spur" brings to this text. I get the image of a horse barely moving along. After receiving the swift kick of the cowboy's spur, the horse jolts into action. Let's encourage others with our words, spurring each other to finish the race strongly.

Created to Glorify

"Because Your love is better than life, my lips will glorify You. I will praise
You as long as I live, and in Your name I will lift up my hands." —Psalm 63:3–4

THIS WEEK WE HAVE LOOKED at a long list of "dos" and "don'ts'" as we speak. If you are like me, I find that sometimes rules can get a little overwhelming. Please remember that being a follower of Jesus is not about a list of rules and regulations. It is about a relationship. God sent His one and only Son, Jesus, to take the payment for our sins. If we believe in Him, we can enjoy heaven with Him through eternity (John 3:16). He blesses us (yes, blesses us!) with rules as guidelines for our own protection and to help further His Kingdom. He wants us to obey Him. It is not supposed to be a burden or chore.

Think of it this way…Let's say you purchased a new board game to play with your family. After you opened the box, you could not find the instructions. Would you still play? You could try to make some rules up, but it will inevitably end up with conflict of some sort. When that does not work, you could just give up knowing that you will never get it right on your own. That is when you flip over the box and see a website where the directions for the game can be downloaded online. They were there the whole time, you just had not been paying attention. Without instruction there is chaos. With instruction there is guidance and purpose (and even a little fun)! Guarding your mouths is not meant to be a chore or a burden. It is meant to give blessing and encouragement.

In Matthew 11:28–30, Jesus shares, "Come to Me, all you who are weary and burdened, and I will give you rest. Take My yoke upon you and learn from Me, for I am gentle and humble in heart, and you will find rest for your souls. For My yoke is easy and My burden is light." He loves us and has our very best in mind.

Look up Psalm 63:3–4. Why does David want to use his lips to praise?

Our lips glorify God because He loves us, not because He forces us to love Him. We praise Him with sincere hearts full of gratitude and appreciation. In the fourth week of our study, we referenced 1 John 4:10. It says, "This is love: not that we loved God, but that He loved us and sent His Son as an atoning sacrifice for our sins."

We obey out of our love for Him because He loved us first (1 John 4:19)! If our hearts are filled with His love, we will desire to share it with others. Let us use our mouths to spread His love and glory to others!

The church at Corinth had been receiving unscriptural doctrine from false teachers that Paul needed to clarify. People were still trying to live under the Law of Moses and not under the New Covenant of Christ's sacrifice. The Law had a time and place, but it had been made complete in Jesus. It was part of God's sovereign plan to show us that we could not keep the Lord's commandments, no matter how hard we tried. It revealed to us our need for a Savior.

Keep the purpose of the Old Testament law in mind as you look up 2 Corinthians 3:9–11 and write it in your own words below. (If you are reading the NIV translation, the "ministry that condemns man" is referring to the Law).

We are no longer under the Law, but under the New Covenant. How much more glorious is the ministry that writes on the tablets of human hearts instead of on stone (2 Corinthians 3:3)? God loves us. Our mouths should be telling this truth and proclaiming the glory of God until He returns. Telling of God's saving grace is one way to give Him the glory.

Paul has one final word to say about using our mouths to glorify God. Fill in the blanks below using Romans 15:5–6 (NIV).

"May the God who gives endurance and _____ give you

a spirit of _____ among yourselves as you follow Christ Jesus,

so that with _____ _____ and _____ you may

_____ the God and Father of our Lord Jesus Christ."

May we unite as followers of Christ to encourage, build up, instruct, love, and proclaim the love of God to bring Him the glory.

WEEK SIX

The Hands of a Servant: Utilizing Your Gifts

Day One: Stepping Out of Your Comfort Zone (2 Corinthians 12:9)

Day Two: The Heart of a Servant (Ephesians 6:7)

Day Three: Going the Extra Mile (Matthew 5:41)

Day Four: Growing Weary (2 Thessalonians 3:13)

Day Five: Purposeful Pruning (John 15:1–6)

Challenge Thought:

Would you rather serve or be served? Too often, believers approach church with a "what can it do for me" mentality, when it should be the exact opposite! We fill our churches with programs that appease the masses. We have youth programs, Bible drill teams, Christian concerts, potlucks, scrapbooking circles, choir practice, and so forth. You get the point. God can work in and through any of these as He chooses; however, it may be time to spend as much time serving *outside* of the church as we do sitting *inside* of the church. Ephesians 4:11–13 teaches that we are equipped to serve, not equipped to sit in the audience. This week will be looking at how to utilize the gifts God has given us by serving others.

DAY ONE

Stepping Out of Your Comfort Zone

"...My grace is sufficient for you, for my power is made perfect in weakness."
—2 Corinthians 12:9

FOR THE PAST FIVE YEARS, my life has been tossed around to the point that I do not even remember what a comfort zone is. I have moved across the country (twice!), have lived in four different homes, and have gone from a full-time working woman to a full-time stay-at-home mom with two children. Life keeps changing right before my eyes. Despite all of the discomfort that comes with change, it has been a great opportunity to grow! The idea of stepping out of my comfort zone is not quite as intimidating as it once was.

If serving others is out of your comfort zone, you are not alone. I urge you, however, to step out in faith. It is only when we are out of our comfort zone that we truly learn to rely on God's strength instead of our own.

This week will be focusing on who we should serve, why we should serve, how we are to serve, what serving is, how to balance your schedule, and how your past might influence where you serve. First of all, let's look into what the Scriptures have to say about who we should serve.

Joshua challenges us to choose this day whom we will serve. Check out Joshua 24:15. Who did Joshua's family choose to serve?

Read Galatians 5:13 and 6:10. Who do these verses say that we should serve?

I particularly appreciate the emphasis on loving other believers. Do not miss that. Put your brothers- and sisters-in-Christ first. I will not expound too much here, but a dysfunctional church family is not reaching its fullest potential on so many levels. Ephesians 4:11–13 says that serving builds up the church.

These verses call us to serve God and serve others. Serving man is an easy way to experience burnout, for humans will let us down. They will not always say "thank you." They will not always appreciate what we do. I am certain you have experienced this a time or two (or 200)!

What does Colossians 3:23–24 say about this?

You may be serving men, but they are not your masters. You must remember that you are not serving to please man, but to bring glory to God. If you start trying to please others, you will fail. We all need this reminder every now and then.

Why should we serve God and serve others? Before we look into this more, please record your initial thoughts about this question.

Take a few minutes to look up four passages and record what each verse says should be our motive when serving.

1 Samuel 12:24

2 Chronicles 15:7

Romans 12:1

Hebrews 6:10

You might go to church every week, raise your kids with love, teach Sunday school, facilitate a small group in your home, and feed the homeless twice a month. As you serve, remember that good works do not get you into Heaven. Even though we might do good things for God, our sin still separates us from Him. We need to ask for His forgiveness and for His free gift of salvation. It is then (and only then) that you will inherit eternity with Him and will truly be able to have a relationship with Him. In Him, you will be made righteous (2 Corinthians 5:21).

If you are a believer, God approves of you, not because of what He sees you doing, but because He sees Who is in you. Trying to earn His love and forgiveness never works. You cannot get to heaven because you are a "good person." Think of Paul (a murderer) and Rahab (a prostitute). Even by "worldly standards" they were not "good" people, yet they are people who are still remembered today because of the great faith and courage they displayed after obeying God. Have you asked Jesus to forgive you from your sins? If so, take a moment and thank God for all that He has done for you. If not, what better time than now?

I want you to truly think about whether or not you are ready for the next level of serving God, even if you are feeling unqualified. The idea may be a little intimidating, so let me share a little analogy that might be of encouragement.

> *Imagine that God wants to teach you how to skydive. He encourages you to just get in the plane; and you obey, not sure how this is going to end.*

> *You are soaring high above the earth, and the door slowly creaks open. To your surprise, God does not tell you to jump. He simply invites you to look out and enjoy the beauty of creation. You peer over the edge, still a bit uneasy.*

> *Then He whispers to you, "Just try on the parachute." Easy enough. You put on the parachute. You look over the edge again. "I am not going to push you," God reminds you, smiling. "I will wait until you are ready."*

There you are. You have taken lots of small baby steps to get to this point.

You have stepped onto the plane, peered out the door, and tried on the parachute. God has equipped you with everything you need. He is ready when you are.

"But God," you find yourself saying. "I can't do this on my own."

"You are right, my dear child. I am going with you. I will be there the whole way. You don't have to worry."

God then proceeds to strap Himself to you and together, you jump out of the plane and you hold on for the ride of your life!

God never intended us to rely on our own strength. That is why He calls you out of your comfort zone; because it is then that you will have to rely on Him. Learning to trust Him is a step-by-step process that is always changing and expanding as you experience Him more and more (and discover for yourself that He is true to His Word). He says "Never will I leave you; never will I forsake you." (Hebrews 13:5) and "My grace is sufficient for you, for My power is made perfect in weakness" (2 Corinthians 12:9).

The Heart of a Servant

"Serve wholeheartedly, as if you were serving the Lord, not men."
—Ephesians 6:7

YESTERDAY WE LEARNED ABOUT "WHO" we should serve and "why" we should serve, now let's look at the "how." There are really two pieces to the how we are to serve—*internal* and *outward*. Let's take a quick look at the *internal* first. When it comes to serving, the topic of our hearts returns once more. Look up the verses below and record what you discover.

Galatians 5:13

Ephesians 6:7–8

Romans 12:11

We are to serve wholeheartedly and in love, just like our Master. We are to serve with zeal and enthusiasm! 1 Peter 5:5 adds another look into our hearts. I love the way the New Living Translation words it. Please read it below.

> "In the same way, you younger men must accept the authority of the elders. And all of you, serve each other in humility, for 'God opposes the proud but favors the humble.'"

Go back and circle the word that tells how we are to serve. Humility is totally selfless and is giving in nature. In John 13:12–17, we see Jesus' example of how He selflessly served others on earth.

What had Jesus just finished doing in the verses prior to this passage?

Now flip over a few pages in your Bible to John 15:13. What does this verse say Christ did out of His love for us?

There is no doubt that Christ is the ultimate picture of a true servant. Is it not exciting that we have some awesome examples of everyday servants in the Bible to follow as well? There were men and women that gave up their plans to follow Christ. These examples were sinners—just like us. Still, through it all, they did not seek human applause; but they desired to hear "well done" at the end of their life's journey (Matthew 25:21).

Inwardly, we are to serve in humility and love with our whole hearts. Now we will move on to the *outward* ways we are to serve. There are few New Testament verses that refer to this outward act of service, commonly referred to as "Spiritual Gifts." Today will be narrowing it down to two of them. Please read the passages below written by Paul and Peter. Then list out the gifts that the Scripture verses reference.

Romans 12:6–8

1 Peter 4:7–11

Go back and reread the list. *Circle any gifts that you have.* If you are a believer, you do have a gift of some sort!

> What are the gifts for and how are they to be used? (To find the answer, check out 1 Corinthians 12:7 and 1 Peter 4:10–11.)

The purpose of gifts is to help build up the church or the body of believers. We are one body with many parts (gifts). In 1 Corinthians 12:21, Paul shows how important each part is to the body. The eye needs the hand, and the head needs the feet. He says that both are "indispensable."

God arranged everyone's gifts, just as He wanted them to be and gave you a gift that is unique and, most importantly, needed. You are Christ's workmanship (Ephesians 2:10). It is time to get to work!

DAY THREE

Going the Extra Mile

"If someone forces you to go one mile, go with him two miles."
—Matthew 5:41

THE FOLLOWING IS AN EXCERPT from the book, *Concentric Circles of Concern*. The book talks about making an impact for Christ where we are and how those we impact can impact others—much like a rock sending ripples far out into the water.

I look out into a field and see a Jewish boy doing some pruning in the vineyard. It was a Roman law in those days that the soldiers could ask the Jews to carry their baggage for one mile.

A Roman soldier comes along and says, "Boy, come here. I want you to carry my baggage."

The infuriated Jewish boy, with white knuckles and clenched teeth climbs over the fence. As he climbs over, he knocks some rocks off the fence, which angers him even more. If looks could kill! Well, he picks up the baggage but does not say a thing. When he comes to the end of that mile, he drops that baggage like a hot rock, turns on his heels, and returns to his work in the vineyard.

The next day, the Roman passes by the same vineyard. He looks out and sees someone he thinks is the same boy and decides to aggravate him again. The Roman soldier says, "Boy, come and carry my baggage again."

The boy looks up and says, "Good morning, sir," bolts the fence, picks up the baggage, and says, "What is your destination?"

The Roman soldier says, "I am going to Caesarea. I am going back to Rome."

"Do you have family?" the boy asks.

"Yes," says the Roman soldier. "A wife and three children."

The boy involves the Roman in conversation. They come to the end of the first mile. The Roman sees it; the Jewish boy ignores it.

Finally, the boy and the Roman come to the end of the second mile. The boys says, "Well, I must get back to my work."

The Roman says, "Son, didn't you see the mile marker back there? You went two miles."

"Oh," the boy says, "I know. But my master says, 'Whoever shall force you to go one mile, go with him two.'"

But you say, "That is going to cost me."

I ask you, "Did it cost Jesus to go to the cross?"

Remember, love is an action. It is doing. It is meeting needs. Our attitude is formed on the immediacy of who is in control—Jesus or me. I form an attitude, and out of that attitude, I react.[14]

Look up the words that Jesus spoke in Matthew 5:41. What does this verse mean to you after reading the story above?

---

[14] Thompson, W. Oscar and Carolyn Thompson Ritzmann. *Concentric Circles of Concern: Seven Stages for Making Disciples.* Nashville: B&H Publishing, 1999, pp. 156-157.

We need to go above and beyond the call of duty. As we learned yesterday, we are not serving men; we are serving God.

> Can you think of a time when you did more than was expected of you? I am sure you put forth much effort, but did you find any satisfaction in knowing that you did your best? How does this action bring glory to God?

After learning to recognize the Holy Spirit (as seen in week one), you will become more aware of what God is asking you to do. Our task is simply to obey. If you delay obedience, you might also have delayed results.

Several years ago, I volunteered to help make cupcakes for a concession stand. The proceeds were going to help dig a well in a small African village where they had no clean water. My friend who was leading up the whole operation was going to the village that fall. She wanted to meet the people in the village and tell them about the God who was providing for their needs. All that to say, I could have made two dozen cupcakes. It would have been helpful and not much work for me at all. I decided to do a bit more. We did not have a lot of extra money at the time; but, fortunately, cupcakes did not cost much to make. They took time to decorate, but I had some free time to give. I was able to make about eight dozen cupcakes. I remember that the first four dozen were very easy and painless; but after decorating the entire batch, my hands were sore. I was ready to be done. I will never forget the look on her face when I handed her the cupcakes. She said, "You did way too much work!" I looked up and her and said (without even thinking), "Two dozen would have been easy giving. Eight dozen—for me—was sacrificial giving." Needless to say, my few dollars that I invested yielded over $100 in profits for the villagers. It is a lesson I will never forget.

Please understand my heart: I do not write this story to brag. If I share a story with you, it is to encourage you and give God the glory. I would love to write about how I was singing praises the whole time I was working, but that was not the case! It was not an easy task for me, and it was labor-intensive. I can tell you, however, that I did my very best and went above and beyond what I was asked to do; and it felt great! A sore hand and a few lost hours were a small price to pay. I was also able to practice changing out negative thoughts for positive ones.

God is not looking for capability, He is looking for availability. God is looking for willing bodies. He will provide you with everything else you need to complete whatever task He would like you to do. He has already been equipping you for the specific ministry He has in mind for you. Are you willing to be His servant and to go the extra mile for His glory?

Growing Weary

"As for you, brothers, never tire of doing what is right."
—2 Thessalonians 3:13

O N THE SPECTRUM OF SERVING, there are two sides. On one end, we stay focused on ourselves and make up excuses to avoid serving. On the other end, we are run ragged and are growing weary. We are so busy serving others that we do not leave room for God to work.

If I had to guess, most believers are not looking for a place to serve. They probably are already serving. For many of you, yesterday's lesson probably was not applicable to where you are at the moment. If I had to guess, many of you are already serving in more than one place...or two.

Be very cautious of this! Do not be too busy "playing church" to be able to focus on God and where He wants you to be. Growing weary is a topic of which we all need to be aware, and we need constantly asking ourselves, "Are we over-involved?" This is an area where I always have to be on the lookout.

You might be thinking, "Is there really too much of a good thing?" The answer to that question is yes! Today we will be looking at finding the balance of serving. *Spreading yourself too thin can not only wear you out, but it can render you useless in whatever ministry God has called you to do.*

Do you find the statement above to be true in your own life? Perhaps you are currently spreading yourself too thin and are ready for a change. Take a moment to think about this and jot down any thoughts that God reveals in the space below. Allow God to speak to you in a gentle, loving way that only He can do to speak truth into your life.

Satan can use our busy lives to keep us from getting anything with eternal value accomplished. Not only that, but he fools us into believing that we are actually being helpful in each ministry that we are involved. It is a delicate balance that needs to be handled by God.

Look up 2 Thessalonians 3:13 and write it below.

How does this verse tie into what we have been learning?

There is a song by Casting Crowns called "Does Anybody Hear Her?" that has a short, simple, and profound phrase that can easily be overlooked. It says, "She is running 100 miles per hour in the wrong direction."[15] Can you ever relate? If that is you, my friend, put on the brakes and turn around.

You cannot fix everything. You cannot be involved in every ministry. You do not have to be the feet, the ears, *and* the hands of the church. Each believer has a special part to play. Do not take away someone else's opportunity to serve. God will provide a worker. If you are not involved in any way, hurry up! Someone else could use a break!

If you are juggling too many balls, more than likely, you are bound to drop one (if not all of them); and you will probably need some recovery time afterwards. Do not juggle too many things. If you grow weary of "doing good" that is "no good."

There is a little passage from *The Autobiography of George Muller* that reminds us of the danger of growing weary. In it, he writes:

---

[15] Casting Crowns. "Can Anybody Hear Her?" By Mark Hall. *Lifesong.* Beach Street Records, 2005.

"Often the work of the Lord itself may tempt us away from communion with Him. A full schedule of preaching, counseling, and travel can erode the strength of the mightiest servant of the Lord. Public prayer will never make up for closest communion."[16]

In other words, if you find that you have enough time to be involved in the church and other good acts of service but not enough time to be involved in one-on-one time with God, it is time to stop and regroup.

If this description sounds like you, it is time to make some changes. If the Holy Spirit is convicting you in this area, it is time to start praying and seeking godly counsel about what to eliminate so that you can start to have some alone time with God and His Word. You need time this time of quiet and reflection to maintain your sanity. Do not approach it with a "have to" but with a "get to" mentality. It should not be a burden. Just remember that "man shall not live on bread alone, but on every word that comes from the mouth of God" (Matthew 4:4).

---

16   Muller, pp. 47-48.

Purposeful Pruning

"I am the true vine, and My Father is the gardener. He cuts off every branch
in Me that bears no fruit, while every branch that does bear fruit He prunes so
that it will be even more fruitful. You are already clean because of the words
I have spoken to you. Remain in Me, and I will also remain in you. No branch
can bear fruit by itself; it must remain in the vine. Neither can you bear fruit
unless you remain in Me. I am the vine; you are the branches. If you remain in
Me and I in you, you will bear much fruit; apart from Me you can do nothing. If
you do not remain in Me, you are like a branch that is thrown away and withers;
such branches are picked up, thrown into the fire and burned." —John 15:1–6

TODAY'S PASSAGE IS RICH WITH application. There is a gardener, a vine, pruned branches, discarded branches, and fruit. We learn that the gardener (God) is responsible for pruning. We learn that the branches (people) are to remain in the vine (Jesus). Those who do not produce fruit, are thrown in the fire to be burned. Those who stay attached to the vine will be pruned so they bear even more fruit. Today we will be simply learning more about how the process of pruning is beneficial for bearing more fruit and bringing God the glory.

As we begin today's lesson, take a look at your own life. Have you ever felt like you were up against an overwhelming task that you knew God was calling you to do? How did it make you feel?

Have you ever stopped to think that maybe the task was too much for you to handle? Maybe God gives you that task so that you learn to rely on Him.

Your past (whether good, bad, or a combination of the two) fuels your future. It is oftentimes during times of trial and suffering that God reveals or even refines His gifts to us. For me, personally, frequently moving and trying to get to know people in new locations have refined my hospitality skills.

> How about you? How has God used a hard thing in your life to help build up a spiritual gift in you? We tend to go to the most recent events in our life, but try to think back over the course of your lifetime as well.

Not only did moving refine my skills, but it also helped define me as a person. As I was looking through some of my old writings, I discovered this little snippet in one of my journals from a few years ago. It said:

> *He moved me here to encourage me to slow down. He took away everything to show me how much I needed Him. He was and is the only One who can get me through. When others are too busy, He is not. He did not leave me with nothing. Instead, because I obeyed, He blessed me even more than I ever had been before or ever imagined that I could be.*

Since writing this, my family and I have once again packed up all of our belongings and moved across the country; and do you know what? The same is still true. I believe this statement more now, because I have another trial under my belt through which God has pulled me.

Times of hardship are just logs that help fuel the fire of growth within us. We need them (yes…"need" them!) to mature and to gain wisdom. Storms, tidal waves, and sharks are necessary to help strengthen our faith. If God has helped you to overcome one obstacle, chances are, the next time you face another one, the trial will not feel so overwhelming. That is what growing is all about!

Please read John 15:5 on the next page and *circle the word that describes what we are able to accomplish without God's help.*

"I am the vine; you are the branches. If a man remains in Me and I in him, he will bear much fruit; apart from Me you can do nothing."

We need to remain in God to be effective in ministry. If you do not have a servant's heart, you will end up frustrated and will eventually quit. Keep in mind that in order for a plant to bear fruit, it must first be pruned. Pruning hurts, but it brings great reward. Are you not thankful that the One who is pruning knows you so well?

Now read John 15:8. In this passage, what is said to bring glory to God?

What is a disciple?

There are many aspects to a disciple and many adjectives that describe such a person. You may have words such as, "loyal," "follower," "devoted," or "student." Will you accept the fact that pruning is necessary for growth so that you can be a more effective servant for God's glory? Do not be ashamed of your past. Do not dread upcoming trials. They are all fuel for the fire. It is time throw off everything that entangles you and let your little light shine for His glory!

Week Seven

Put On Your Running Shoes: Persevering and Sharing Your Faith

Day One: Not There Yet (Hebrews 12:1)

Day Two: Commissioned to Go Fishin' (Matthew 28:18–20)

Day Three: Testify (Acts 20:24)

Day Four: God's Wisdom (1 Corinthians 1:17–18)

Day Five: Your Running Buddy (Matthew 5:14–16)

Challenge Thought:

Have you ever considered yourself to be "a runner?" Some of you may, in fact, be runners. However, if you are a follower of Christ, the Scriptures refer to the Christian life as a race (Hebrews 12:1). We may not always know the duration of the race, but we are called to be patient and persevere. We are challenged to share our faith with others whom we encounter on our journey. We are encouraged to run in God's strength and not our own. God even provides us with other "running buddies" along the way. In our seventh and final week, we will be looking at several verses that show us how we are to run the race. Are you ready? Put on those running shoes!

Day One

Not There Yet

"Therefore, since we are surrounded by such a great cloud of witnesses, let us throw off everything that hinders and the sin that so easily entangles, and let us run with perseverance the race marked out for us." —Hebrews 12:1

S EVERAL YEARS AGO, I RECEIVED a disturbing e-mail joke in my inbox. It said: "Why do old people read the Bible?" The answer: "Because they are studying for the big test." Really? Life is the test! The most recent statistics say that one out of every one individuals is going to die (and death does not always save itself for the elderly). The odds are not in humanity's favor. We will be held accountable for how we used the time that God gave us on earth. The test is not given after death, as this "joke" suggests. The test is here and now. Our grade will be based on whether or not we allowed Christ to take the test in our place. It is a pass or fail system.

The Bible is packed full of wisdom for life. Life is one big race. It is more of a marathon than of a sprint. We are to pace ourselves.

Look up Hebrews 12:1–3. What did the verse have to say about our feet? (Hint: How are we to run the race)?

What about our eyes?

What about our hearts?

The race involves much more than just our feet. The journey of life requires us to use our eyes, our hearts, our minds, and our hands—just as we have seen over the course of the past several weeks. It is a race of perseverance and not a race of speed.

Now look up James 1:2–5. In this passage, James is referring to trials as a time of joy. Where do trials lead?

To what does the testing of your faith lead?

What does perseverance bring?

I do not know about you, but I could always use a bit more wisdom and maturity. How do we get wisdom? Verse 5 says "by asking God." However, the passage also suggests that maturity and wisdom are gained through the perseverance that comes from enduring trials. How can we consider the testing of our faith a joyous event? We need to remember that the painful process leads to something greater—God's wisdom and a deeper relationship with Him. We spoke briefly of this last week when we addressed the topic of being pruned to bear fruit.

If you are "stuck" in a trial period of your life right now, what should you do? Look up, not out! God is preparing you for something bigger. Try to take your eyes off your circumstances.

What is God trying to teach you in your current season of life? If you do not know, that is okay. He might not reveal it to you on this side of heaven. If you do know or think you might have an idea, please write it down in the space below. In a few years, you might be looking back at this study and realize that you were right or that He had another, separate lesson to teach you as well.

Commissioned to Go Fishin'

> "Then Jesus came to them and said, 'All authority in heaven and on earth has been given to me. Therefore go and make disciples of all nations, baptizing them in the name of the Father and of the Son and of the Holy Spirit, and teaching them to obey everything I have commanded you. And surely I am with you always to the very end of the age.'" —Matthew 28:18–20

I T IS TIME TO PULL out all of the stops. We can recognize truth, keep our eyes to the skies, think on godly things, love the unlovable, speak in truth and kindness, serve the body of believers, and run the race with perseverance; but we are still not doing all that God called us to do.

Let's begin by looking up Matthew 4:19. Note Jesus' words to His soon-to-be disciples. What does He ask them to do, and what does He call them? (Keep your finger in the text, for we are coming back to it in a minute!)

Now read Matthew 28:18–20 at the top of this lesson (also called the "Great Commission") and record some of Jesus' final words to His followers before ascending back into Heaven.

In these verses, Jesus challenges us to use all that we have learned to go and share the Gospel with others. We are to become "fishers of men."

> Reread Matthew 4:19. What do you think Jesus meant by the phrase "fishers of men"?

We have been commissioned to go fishin'! The things we have studied until now are all good things, but this lesson is the glue that holds them all together. Non-believers can be kindhearted and speak in love. They are just as capable at serving as we are. The difference is this: We are to attach the name of God and His one and only Son to everything we do.

Are you "lucky" to have a good job in today's economy, or have you been blessed by God with a place of work? Was your surgeon able to come up with a solution to your ailment, or was it God's hand helping to heal your body? Was it by chance that your children turned out "okay," or was it by God's grace? Did you make the best choice for your family, or was it God giving you wisdom to make the best choice for your family?

Is God encouraging you to get out of your comfort zone and start fishing? If you are a follower, then the answer is yes! It is time to get off the shores, into the water, and start fishin'!

DAY THREE

Testify

"However, I consider my life worth nothing to me, if only I may finish the race and complete the task the Lord Jesus has given me—the task of testifying to the gospel of God's grace." —Acts 20:24

WHY IS IT SO DIFFICULT to keep a secret? Have you ever been told some little piece of news that you were told to keep a secret? Can you imagine what it would have been like if Jesus had said that we were to keep the Good News to ourselves? That sounds crazy, yet how often do we really share our faith with others? Do we share it as it is meant to be shared? The Gospel is not a secret! We are meant to share it with all people and to proclaim the resurrection.

Check out the following verses. What does each one say about sharing the Gospel? Record your thoughts in the space provided.

Luke 9:60

Acts 5:42b

1 Peter 3:15–16

Do you share with urgency? Is your witnessing surrounded by prayer? Are you consistently sharing your faith? Are you prepared to give gentle and respectable answers? If the answer to any of these is "no," you may want to find out why you are not doing these things.

The more you know, the more you will grow. The more you grow, the more inclined you will be to share. Why? Because God's love is exciting! It is rewarding and fulfilling. It is like nothing else that you have ever experienced. Once you have felt it, you will not want to keep it a secret.

Now look up Mark 8:38. How does the author suggest we are to share the Gospel?

1 Timothy 2:3–6 sheds more light on the topic. What does this passage say that God desires (particularly in verse 4)?

As I was researching different topics for this study, I came across an old journal of mine with an interesting excerpt that I would like to share. It was written my senior year of high school, which—looking back—was right at the end of a few challenging years in my life. It was interesting to see the faith that I had been taught since I was a child and how it carried me through adulthood. In this particular entry, I was convicted to be more open in my faith.

April 10th

> *Life—how easily we take it for granted. When I get to heaven, one of the questions I'll ask Jesus is why He chooses some and not others and how He knows when to do it.*
>
> *Tonight my mom informed me that one of my old classmates was found dead on the job. I didn't know him, but I can't imagine how many times I must have passed him in the halls. He must have been the quiet type—I didn't even recognize his picture. He was one out of a dozen seniors that I don't know. This time, the Lord spared my emotions.*

One thing I wonder, though, was the matter of salvation. Was he saved? What if he saw me in the halls? What if he never saw Christ in me and I made no effort to tell him? It challenges me to be more open about my faith, especially when I realize how short our days here on earth really are.

In 1 Corinthians 15:22–23, Paul writes, "For as in Adam all die, so in Christ all will be made alive. But to each his own turn." Because man is a sinner, we all must face the consequence—death (Romans 6:23) and yet I know, as a Christian, I'll be having one awesome eternal party. I just hope that I can hand out enough invitations before the big event arrives!

Lord, thank you for your mercy on this earthly soul. Help me to live each day to its fullest and share you with others. Amen.

That was a pretty loaded journal entry for a high schooler. I look back now and can see those little steps God put in my life to help draw me into a closer relationship with Him. I wonder what it will be like in ten years looking back to where I am now. By God's grace, I will be a woman who clings to Acts 20:24 (NIV). Please look up the passage and use it to fill in the blanks below.

"…I consider my life worth _____ to me, if only I may finish the

_____ and complete the task the Lord Jesus has given me—the task of

_____ to the _____ of God's grace."

My prayer is the same for you! Testify the Good News of the Gospel in order to bring glory to God our Father. Besides, as Richard Stearns from World Vision put it, "Two thousand years ago, the world was changed forever just by twelve [disciples]."[17] All it took was twelve men to testify God's love to impact the entire world with the Gospel message.

---

[17]   Stearns, Richard. *A Hole in the Gospel.* Nashville, TN: Thomas Nelson Publishers, 2009, p. 5.

God's Wisdom

"For Christ did not send me to baptize, but to preach the gospel—not with words of human wisdom, lest the cross of Christ be emptied of its power. For the message of the cross is foolishness to those who are perishing, but to us who are being saved it is the power of God." —1 Corinthians 1:17–18

THERE IS NO MAGIC NUMBER of how many times a person must hear the Gospel before she comes to a decision to accept Christ for herself. It could be the first time she hears. It could be that she hears it a hundred times and takes her unbelief with her to the grave. We do not know. God does. That is why it is so essential to be able to be a vessel that He can use. You may not realize how your words are impacting someone for Christ if you are not there to see them through to their decision.

How about you? If you are a believer and follower of Christ, roughly how many times did you hear about Christ before you accepted Him?

Keep at it! Do not be discouraged by someone for whom you have been praying for years who has not made a decision. It could be any day now. Keep praying. If you have been teaching your children about God's love and they have not yet accepted Him, keep praying. (Do you see a pattern developing here?) Put it in His hands. He has perfect timing, and it just is not the right time yet. Be patient.

> Have you ever avoided sharing Christ with someone because you were afraid of saying the wrong thing or because you were not "theological" enough? Share any experiences that come to mind below.

John 14:26 will help take away the pressure! What does it say?

Sometimes I need to remind myself that I am not the one leading their hearts. It is the Holy Spirit's work. You may have heard that "Amateurs built the ark; professionals built the Titanic." If God is for you, who can be against you (Romans 8:31)?

> Please turn to 1 Corinthians 1:17 and sum up the passage in your own words in the space below.

Do you realize that the disciples were as human as we are (and younger, too)? They did not have the Bible or commentaries to read before going out and sharing the Gospel. That did not stop the message from spreading like wildfire. The Holy Spirit can work in ways that we cannot.

Have you been relying on your own strength to share the Gospel with someone? God already knows, so go ahead and confess it to Him. He is waiting with open arms and ready to forgive you. He is ready to take over so that you no longer have to rely on yourself. Trust me—He is much better at it than we ever could be, and He is never too busy to handle even the smallest things. Never cease to share your faith in words and deeds. Colossians 3:17 says that "...whatever you do, whether in word or deed, do it all in the name of the Lord Jesus, giving thanks to God the Father through Him."

In closing, please look up Isaiah 6:8 and write out the words of the verse below. Feel free to write some of them in bold letters if you feel so inclined.

Your Running Buddy

"You are the light of the world. A city on a hill cannot be hidden. Neither do people light a lamp and put it under a bowl. Instead they put it on its stand, and it gives light to everyone in the house. In the same way, let you light shine before men, that they may see your good deeds and praise your Father in heaven."
—Matthew 5:14–16

I HAVE TO SMILE. THE LAST day of our study has snuck upon us. I am so blessed that you chose to stick it out until the end. I am quite certain that by now you have laughed (and potentially cried) as you opened your heart to the Holy Spirit. Most importantly, you have hopefully been encouraged to take your faith to the next step. I am certain that the Lord has moved in your heart as you have grown over the past several weeks.

It is time now for the great send-off—the "Great Commission," if you will. I pray that the Lord revealed Himself to you time and time again while you were faithfully seeking Him. I pray that He placed a hunger in you that will never be satisfied unless you are in close fellowship with Him.

I pray that you use what you have learned and that you do not keep this knowledge to yourself. I pray that you share with others what God has taught you in order for Him to receive the glory. After all, has this not been the focus of this entire study?

Ladies, the fields are ripe with harvest, but the workers are few (Matthew 9:37). Get out there, start sharing the Good News with others, and use all that you have been given to give glory back to the One Who made you!

Stick together. If you are doing this as a small group study, then the Lord has blessed you with an amazing group of ladies who will help you on your journey through life. Remember that God is always with you, and you are never alone (Hebrews 13:5). However, I encourage you to find a spiritual "running buddy" (or several) to keep you on track. Intentionally position yourself next to godly women who are good role models. They just might "rub off" on you!

Please look up one final Scripture to end our time together. It is found in Matthew 5:14–16. Write it in your own words.

Who spoke these words?

To whom was He speaking?

I am going to write the verses a little differently to help capture the message. Do not forget to fill in the blank with your name!

Dear _____, *(your name)*

"*You are the light of the world…let your light shine before others, that they may see your good deeds and glorify your Father in Heaven.*"

Love,

Jesus

P.S. Whatever you do, do it for the glory of God!

Preparation for Leaders

You are about to embark on an awesome adventure with a wonderful group of women. Whether you are a first time facilitator or a "seasoned pro," my prayer for you is that this study not only causes the other ladies to pursue the next level on their walk with Christ but that you, too, are challenged by the Scriptures. Cover your time each week in prayer. Expect hiccups along the way—not only in the group, but in your personal life as well. Satan wants to keep you from building the Kingdom. It is time to strap on your armor (Ephesians 6) and dive into God's Word as we shed some light onto how God created us to bring Him glory. Here are a few pointers to help you as you prepare each week.

- Open and close your time together each week with prayer. Invite God to encourage, challenge, and guide as you work through the Scriptures.
- Allow the ladies to get to know each other. They will not begin to share openly until a certain level of trust is built. Some may never "open up"—and that is okay. Just because their mouths are not moving, does not mean that God is not stirring their hearts. The first week, encourage them to introduce themselves (perhaps to the group). Make nametags to avoid awkwardness for those who are horrible at remembering names. Have a little group game or "mixer." You can find some ideas online. These are just a few ways that you can "warm up" the group.
- Do not feel the need to teach. Your job is simply to facilitate. Go through the questions and invite the ladies to share what God has laid on their hearts. Be prepared to share your own story. Sometimes it just takes one authentic answer for others to feel safe to open up as well. Be an example.
- There will be days when you want to quit or cut corners. There will be also be days that the women in your group will want to quit or cut corners. When those times come, cling to these promises:

"He gives strength to the weary and increases the power of the weak." —Isaiah 40:29

"So do not fear, for I am with you; do not be dismayed, for I am your God. I will strengthen you and help you; I will uphold you with my righteous right hand." —Isaiah 41:10

- Ultimately, there is nothing that either you or I can do in our own strength to draw people to God. He must do that Himself. Hopefully that takes some of the pressure off you. We can, however, point them to God's Word (Hebrews 4:12). Encourage the ladies in your group to bring a Bible (either digital or hardcopy) with them each week. Spend time reading some of the Scriptures in the lessons together. At the beginning of each day, you will see a key verse or passage for that lesson. You may wish to challenge the group to handwrite these verses each day on a 3x5 notecard. At the end of the study, they will have a total of 35 Bible passages written out on cards that can be placed around their homes.
- Most importantly, have fun! There is a time to cry, but there is also a time to laugh (Ecclesiastes 3)! Remember that "whatever you do, do it all for the glory of God" (1 Corinthians 10:31b). You are salt. You are a light (Matthew 5). You, my friend, were CREATED TO GLORIFY!